BOTHIE THE POLAR DOG

British Library Cataloguing in Publication Data
Fiennes, Ranulph
  Bothie the polar dog.
  1. Transglobe Expedition (*1979–1982*)
  2. Bothie (Dog)
  I. Title   II. Fiennes, Virginia
  910.4'1   G420.T7

  ISBN 0 340 36319 3

Bothie wants to dedicate this
book to all his Transglobe friends
and Blackdog

CONTENTS

	To the Ends of the Earth	13
1	Bothie Volunteers for the Team	15
2	Bothie Breaks the Ice	27
3	Digging in on a Catless Continent	44
4	Bothie of the Antarctic	53
5	Forbidden Dog at the South Pole	70
6	Dog Days on the Yukon	88
7	Bothie in Love	108
8	North Pole and Home	121

MAPS

	page
The Transglobe Expedition	10–11
Antarctica	47
The Arctic	107

ACKNOWLEDGMENTS

Bothie would like to thank all those people who made 1979–82 so memorable, looked after him and put up with him. In particular he would like to thank Jean Windeler who made two of his polar suits and Spacecoat who made the third; David Mason who taught him many useful tricks; Monique Mason and Jenny Wake-Walker who tolerated his wickedness for many weeks; Terry Kenchington and Howard Willson who whiled away many a happy hour on the MV *Benjamin Bowring*; David Hicks who gave him bones from the galley; Otto Steiner, Les Davis, Cyrus Balaporia, Ken Cameron, John Parsloe, David Peck, Mick Hart, Jim Young, Geoff Lee, Nick Wade, Nigel Cox, Jill Bowring, Eddie Pike, Martin and Annie Weymouth, Edwin Martin, Paul Clark, Chris McQuaid, Lesley Rickett and Anton Bowring – the rest of the ship's crew, who played many and wondrous shipboard ball games and tolerated him and his misdemeanours with good humour; Ollie, Charlie, Simon, Anto, Gerry, Giles and Karl who did likewise in the base camps; all in the London office who arranged resupply of his favourite items throughout the world; Pedigree Petfoods who provided the most delicious and nutritious food for him during the expedition and sent him to the best quarantine kennels; Liz Cartledge, Jane Miller and all the kennel maids at Ruislip Kennels who kept him amused for six months; Flo for getting him home safely; Mike Hoover and Beverley Johnson who recorded his every move on celluloid, taught him many new and mysterious games and kept a warm bed for him in their hut where he was guaranteed a tummy scratch; Peter Booth for finding him in the first place; Maggie Body, who edited out the more unsavoury parts of this story, for her unfailing encouragement in the writing of the book; George Greenfield his literary agent; and Hodder & Stoughton for publishing the adventures of his three years with the Transglobe expedition.

Finally Bothie would like to thank all the many people around the world who welcomed him in South Africa, Sanae, the South Pole, Scott Base, New Zealand, Australia, Los Angeles, and the Canadians of British Columbia, the Yukon, the North West Territories and the Arctic islands.

The authors would also like to acknowledge all the above mentioned and to apologise if Bothie has omitted anyone by name – he is inclined to be a little scatterbrained, but he will always remember you when you meet him again.

PICTURE CREDITS

The authors and publisher wish to thank the following for permission to reproduce their photographs:

Bryn Campbell for 'The welcoming committee at Sanae', 'Old games, new surfaces', 'First up the gangplank at Scott Base', 'Scott's Hut at Cape Evans' and 'Ran-hauling off the Mackenzie River'.

Simon Grimes for 'Dawn patrol against the devil dog of Ryvingen'.

Laurence Howell (Flo) for 'Arctic hare, fun to chase; Arctic wolves, sensible to avoid' and 'Simon, Karl and Gerry unloading the Twin Otter at Alert'.

David Mason for 'Looking north across the sea-ice toward the Pole' and 'Easter 1982 at the North Pole'.

Karl Z'berg for 'Our hut is destroyed'.

All other photographs and the jacket photographs were taken by Ranulph and Virginia Fiennes.

ARCTIC
OCEAN

North Pole

Arctic Circle

YUKON

Vancouver

Los Angeles

80°

Alert
(winter
1981–2)

Svalbard

NORTH ATLANTIC

Greenwich (start 2.9.79
finish 29.8.82)

Algiers

SAHARA

INDIAN
OCEAN

Equator

Abidjan

SOUTH ATLANTIC

Saldanha
Bay

Cape Town

0° longitude

SOUTH PACIFIC

Equator

Sydney Auckland
Christchurch
Campbell Island

SOUTHERN OCEAN

Scott Base
80°
South Pole
ANTARCTICA
Sanae, Ryvingen
(winter 1979–80)
Antarctic Circle

0° longitude

3000 km
2000 S.miles

THE TRANSGLOBE EXPEDITION

11

Don't make the mistake of treating your dogs like humans or they'll treat you like dogs.

MARTHA SCOTT
(no relation to Robert Falcon)

INTRODUCTION

To the Ends of the Earth

RAN: One day in 1972, bored with the lot of a London housewife, Ginnie suggested that we go around the world via the Poles. My job, since leaving the Army, aged twenty-six, had been leading expeditions to remote lands, so I did not scoff at her idea quite as readily as most husbands might have. We had no money other than what we earned from books and lectures about previous expeditions, so we agreed that our circumpolar journey must be mounted on a hundred per cent sponsorship basis. That way we couldn't run into debt.

For seven long years, sitting in a London office using a sponsored telephone, we toiled to get food and clothing, equipment and people, insurance and fuel and, later a ship and ski-plane, all at no cost. Since nobody paid us a wage during the seven years, we lectured at night to make a basic living to pay the gas bill. Unpaid volunteers joined us and had to give up their careers, so there was no doubt as to their dedication.

Our thirty-year-old ship had a crew of sixteen and the plan was to sail south through the Atlantic from Greenwich, roughly along the Greenwich Meridian to Antarctica, then up the far side of the world through the Pacific, finally over the top of the world and back to Greenwich. However, obstacles such as the Sahara,

Antarctica and the semi-frozen Arctic Ocean meant we had to form a small land group which the ship would drop off on one side of each obstacle and collect again on the other.

GINNIE: To make up the land group Ran selected two ex-salesmen, Oliver Shepard and Charles Burton, from 129 volunteers after rigorous tests in Snowdonia. The three of them would become the ice group when we got to Antarctica and the Arctic.

Additionally two people would act as the land group's mobile radio base: I was to be the radio operator in this party and my job would be to keep the land group in touch with each other, with the ship, our London office and with the Twin Otter ski-plane for polar resupply. Simon Grimes would be mechanic and cook in the radio base. Our aircraft would be piloted by Antarctic veteran Giles Kershaw, and in the Arctic by the equally experienced Karl Z'Berg. It would be maintained at both Poles by Army aircraft engineer, Gerrard Nicholson.

In 1976 we had gained polar experience travelling for four months over the north Greenland icecap and in 1977 we tried to reach the North Pole. We failed that year but learnt many lessons which were to prove invaluable for the main journey which we now called the Transglobe Expedition.

His Royal Highness, Prince Charles, became our Patron so the expedition lacked but one component – a mascot.

This book is the story of that mascot.

1

Bothie Volunteers for the Team

RAN: We arrived home from the Arctic training in July 1977. In September that year an old expedition friend of ours, Peter Booth, came to stay. He made up his mind that we were too wrapped up in our work and prescribed a friendly dog about the home to bring us back to earth.

He turned up the very next week with a four week old Jack Russell puppy he'd found in the Hampshire village of Longstock. On seeing this bundle of brown-eyed fluff, hardly large enough to fill two hands, Ginnie's heart just melted.

"What a shame, he *is* lovely, but it's no good," she sighed.

"What d'you mean?" Peter was bewildered.

"Well, we can't take on a puppy, can we? We'll be away on the expedition for at least three years."

"So what!" I interrupted. "He can come too. His fur looks thick enough to deal with polar weather."

"He's a long haired version," agreed Peter. "And it'll get thicker in the cold."

Ginnie needed no further persuasion. When Peter left, the furry white sausage was already well established on the sofa having his fat little tummy scratched.

GINNIE: "What shall we call him?" I asked.

"Better call him after Peter."

15

"But he doesn't look like a 'Peter' and no dog deserves to be called plain 'Booth'."

"Something similar then." Ran smiled and reached for his Roget's *Thesaurus*. " 'Booth, Lean-to, Shack, Bothie'. Those are the only alternatives."

For a while we shouted these words at the puppy but he responded negatively to each.

"Well, he's got no preference it seems. It had better be Bothie," decided Ran. "It's got more edge to it than 'Lean-to' or 'Shack'."

Out in the garden we put Bothie on the lawn. He was wobbly on his legs. Although young to have left his mother, he seemed quite self-possessed and took an immediate interest in his surroundings. A black and white cat jumped onto the fence as it had become accustomed to the safety of our quiet garden. Bothie, startled by this apparition, made a noise like a chair squeaking over lino. This was probably the first bark; the effort of it threw him off balance.

The first few weeks were full of fun and Bothie learnt much about the world, including that there were some activities that were *not* allowed in the house. He never agreed with such discipline, and still complies only when he feels like it. There was no way either of us could stay at home, so Bothie began to travel at a very early age, usually in the minivan, but if that was in use collecting equipment, he sat in my shopping basket on the tube or, when we felt a little more confident, in the saddle bag of my old scooter. We padded the bag out with a towel to stop him rolling around too much, and cut a small hole in the lid so he could look out if he wanted to see the sights. From the beginning he hated to miss an opportunity to travel; he would jump into the mini if a door had been left open, or any car that looked as if it might be going

16

somewhere. He became a favourite of milkman, security men and secretaries alike.

Perhaps because we had him so young, Bothie didn't have the usual male-dog trait of wandering, but always stayed close by. He didn't mind the bustle of our office at all, except when trodden on, which was fairly often as the number of volunteers began to increase. He thrived on attention and loved whoever was patting him at the time. His various toys, ruined slippers, gloves, etc., were scattered under desks and he would get impatient if ignored. If he took one of his toys to someone they'd be sure to react – if only to remove it from their knee – and that was the start of a game.

We had built a tin hut in a car park close to the office where the supplies for our three-year expedition were mounting up. Bothie was often to be found there with Ollie or Simon. Charlie had two female Jack Russells at home and was quite fond of the more attractive side of Bothie, but disliked intensely his bad habits – particularly those involving house training.

One morning, Ollie, Charlie, Ran and I were sitting on packing boxes outside the tin hut enjoying the sunshine and sipping cold drinks. Ollie had been working on a skidoo, one of the oversnow vehicles with a track under the driver's seat and a frontal ski. Bothie went and sat expectantly on its seat.

"Well, Bothie looks all set to come," said Ollie.

The task of finding free food for Bothie for the duration of the journey was added to the list. The hairy hound didn't of course know what enormous decisions had been made on his behalf but he was committed to the expedition from an early age and although he increased the chaos of our overcrowded office, he did also add a source of humour and a ready subject for steam letting.

17

RAN: At home Bothie was *not* universally loved. There were eight cats in our cul-de-sac and no other dogs. He brought a new element into the lives of the cats and, to a peripheral extent, their owners, who I'm sure only refrained from throttling the dog in the knowledge they had not long to put up with him. Some of the cats were physically bigger than Bothie even when, at eleven months, he reached his full height. When cornered they taught him respect for extended claw, spitting fang and arched back but, out on the open tarmac or lawn, they always fled, which gave him that blissful thrill of the chase that is the crowning moment of any dog's day.

Enemy number one was Cat Franklin. We shared a garden fence with Stanley Franklin, the newspaper cartoonist. He was, and is, the perfect neighbour: he makes little or no noise himself, ignores what noise we make and allows me to move around his garden in pursuit of lost Bothie balls or to fix the holes Bothie has dug under our joint fence. But his most saintly quality is that of never complaining about the hideous din Bothie makes in his daily, sometimes hourly, skirmishes with the baleful Cat Franklin, Stanley's beautiful and sedate tortoise-shell.

The fence is of chestnut wattle and seven feet high. Cat Franklin scales it with ease and sits on the ridge grinning down at our dog. The latter goes manic, froths at the mouth and dashes himself against the fence. All but the most robust flora has long since been destroyed in the flowerbeds below, as Bothie leaps twice his height and more in his frustration, often landing on his back before launching a new attack, sometimes via the coal bunker which, on a good day, helps his best leaps get to within three feet of the nonchalant ginger tip of Cat Franklin's tantalisingly twitching tail.

GINNIE: From the beginning Bothie behaved the way he

intended to continue. Two personal traits were especially marked. One was a fervent love of ball games, which was endearing (in moderation), and the other, which caused much bad feeling between him and Ran, was an incurable habit of 'marking' his territorial boundaries on any item, at any time of day and in any company. To begin with, and indeed for his first two years, we would sigh and say "Never mind, he'll soon grow out of it", as we used up soda siphon after soda siphon. But he hasn't, and now he's six, which in human terms is forty-two years old!

Like all puppies with any spirit he helped his teeth develop by chewing any morsel of a chewable nature he could get his paws on. He even seemed to have an eye for quality since, if left alone by some crass error in a room with a choice of delicacies, it would be my only pair of good leather shoes he would select for destruction, not a pensioned off boot. If caught red-handed and berated he would growl back, holding on to his booty, for he was quite without shame. We had a few short weeks of peace from this indiscipline when he lost his milk teeth. Impatient to develop his real teeth we found him yanking out the feeble old ones with his paws and leaving them lying on the carpet.

Although golf balls, twigs or any aerodynamic object sufficed for a fetch-and-return session, Bothie was really a rubber fetishist. At first tennis balls were his favourite, but then he learnt that light rubber footballs, although too big to catch in the mouth, could be headed straight back at the thrower. By burying his balls in the garden he learnt he could get new ones from us simply by sitting around apparently ball-less and looking forlorn. Soon he had an inexhaustible collection of large and small rubber balls, for his own special brand of Chinese water torture. When we were working he would drop a ball on the floor so that it bounced – *boing, boing, boing, boing* . . . Ignoring him was difficult, concentration impossible. With a lunge we would grab the ball and shove it on a shelf out of his reach but, within minutes, he was back bouncing a different ball, often newly smeared with earth and Bothie slobber.

Hiding balls was useless if they were rubber, since Bothie could smell rubber like Army sniffers locate explosives. He was uncanny at it. You could lodge a ball high in the fork of a tree, unseen by the little devil and, an hour later you'd see him squatting in the beg position at the tree's base, whining softly and staring upwards, his black nostrils aquiver. If ignored, within two hours he was biting and tearing at the bark in an effort to shake the ball loose, or if it was one particular old apple tree we have, he would be climbing up its gnarled branches. But come hell or high water he didn't allow any ball to be out of his control for much longer than a day.

Humans were not really necessary for a ball game. If they refused all coaxing Bothie could, and did, throw the ball for himself and he spent many happy hours in the garden this way. When that palled and Cat Franklin didn't show up, blackbirds, thrushes, sparrows and pigeons were seen off. Boeings, Concordes and helicopters that came low overhead, two minutes out from Heathrow, were also good sport. Thunderstorms merited a lugubrious wolf-like howl. All in all he liked the sound of his own voice.

By March 1978, life was hectic as never before, a thousand small details not to overlook and important pieces of the great administrative jigsaw falling out of place as fast as others clicked in. Originally Ran had planned on finding an old fishing trawler for the expedition with a crew of half a dozen. Since we knew nothing about ships we advertised for volunteer crew members.

A twenty-two-year-old Danish merchant navy cadet named Poul Andersson and a twenty-eight-year-old Suffolk sea-wanderer, Anton Bowring, applied and were accepted as deck-hands on the Transglobe ship, provided they could find a suitable vessel on which to be deck-hands, the rest of the crew and any required equipment. For depressing months they visited various European docks and found nothing suitable. Then in Canada they found a twenty-seven-year-old polar research vessel, the M.V. *Martin Karlsen*, originally the famous *Kista Dan*.

Loving her was one thing, paying the £750,000 asking price was quite another. But we found a company in London who had given Captain Scott one of his three ships, the *Terra Nova*, some seventy years before. Anton and Ran suggested to them they had a tradition to keep up – and they agreed.

The makers of Spacecoat clothing which utilises the revolutionary SP29 material, pioneered by NASA astronauts, came to measure up the expedition's team for polar suits. They had some trouble with Bothie's measurements and a long correspondence ensued as to whether he would prefer boots attached to the leggings and whether he would prefer his flies to be of Velcro or a plastic zip.

Everyone took three days off for Christmas, although we could ill afford the time. The young Danish sailor, Poul, spent the holiday with us. After a walk in Richmond Park we came home to Christmas dinner and a tree loaded with presents for everyone, including some from Poul's family that had been secretly sent to us as a surprise. He liked playing with Bothie and his new squeaky toys, and Bothie thought the world of him.

Bothie, not only because he knows which side his bread is buttered, made special friends with Ollie and Charlie. As he would soon have to spend long months cooped up miles from anywhere with the two of them and us, it was lucky they got on. Charlie thought for a long time that it was wrong to take Bothie on the expedition. Ollie may have thought so too but never said anything. Because I had been uncertain if it *was* unkind and worried whether the dog would be subjected to conditions he could not take, I took him to see the chief vet of the RSPCA.

He examined Bothie minutely and said he'd never seen such a strong sturdy dog. He had absolutely no hesitation in giving us the go ahead to take him. But he recommended that we should not wrap him in clothes and boots all the time, but allow his own fur to adapt to the cold. He assured me that he would grow a thick coat and lick his nose constantly to keep it warm.

"There's no difference between this dog going to the Antarctic," he assured me, "and the many dogs that I have seen living for years, very happily, in northern Canada where the temperatures range from hot summers to −45° or −50°C in winter."

The vet gave us just two cold weather warnings. Bothie might have a slight problem with his ears, as they have no protective layers of fat and the fur was unlikely to grow more effectively on them. So we should take special care when there was a wind blowing as well as low temperatures. And we should watch him on sea-ice or newly thawed and refrozen ice, as this is often needle sharp and can make the paws sore. The only real problems our encouraging vet could foresee would be during the first three months of the journey through Africa. But I quickly explained that Bothie would join the expedition in South Africa after the tropics were behind us.

He picked up Bothie to have a last look at the little tyke and wish him well. Bothie, as if to say "Thank you – you're a pal", gave him a dozen wet kisses around his ear before scampering off to fetch his biggest ball and show off his prowess at dribbling it around the room.

In the last few months there was little time for team members to take exercise, yet we would soon need to be on top physical form. In an attempt to make people keep fit in their own time, Ran instigated a monthly twenty-lap circuit of the running track in the barracks where we had our office. Members of our volunteer office staff ticked off runners' names against a stopwatch. Ollie, Simon and Ran actually seemed to enjoy the exertion. Others tolerated it, but there were those whose natural tendencies were decidedly non-masochistic and there was a final group – of two – who found the whole process distinctly undignified. Bothie and I would use any subtle excuse to avoid running. Once or twice we were forced to participate and slunk onto the track to try to keep up with the tail-enders for the last two laps. Bothie would look thoroughly fed up. He failed to understand the purpose of running aimlessly round in circles, but he did keep going as long as his mistress, already breathless, kept calling him to catch up.

RAN: Ginnie was a 20-a-day smoker and never managed more than two laps without collapsing on the grass verge, her chest heaving as Bothie licked her face with concern.

The children's TV programme, 'Blue Peter', heard about Bothie's coming expedition (they showed little or no interest in the other members of the team), and asked him for an interview. He was a great success until he chased the programme's kittens across the studio floor. They were still missing at their next cue.

GINNIE: In February 1979, our Patron, HRH Prince Charles, arrived in our newly acquired Twin Otter, at Farnborough's Royal Aircraft Establishment where we had an exhibition of equipment and were to officially announce the expedition's intentions to the press. He met many of

BOTHIE THE POLAR DOG

our sponsors and most of the team, then he very formally shook paws with Bothie who for the first time seemed to be overcome with awe. The Prince made a speech after which our furry friend's was the loudest appreciation to be heard echoing around the hangar as he showed off his squeaky bark.

In April 1979 several of us, including Bothie, drove to Millwall docks in the east end of London to greet the arrival of the old polar research vessel that was to be our expedition ship. Anton and Poul had performed a small miracle by not only finding a suitable ship but also engaging a full crew of qualified merchant navy volunteers, and achieving sponsors for all the necessary marine equipment.

It was a wonderful feeling as the curved bow, battered and scarred from years of work in the Canadian Arctic, turned into the dock and came fully into sight for the first time. At last it seemed that the Transglobe Expedition was a reality.

When they drew alongside the quay Bothie barked a greeting to Anton and Poul who were busy with ropes and winches. We went on board as soon as the gangway was lowered. Bothie cocked his leg against the post at the top and looked up at Anton as if to say, "Well, I've blessed her for you."

A few weeks later the old ship was christened M.V. *Benjamin Bowring* before being refitted for the expedition. But the small miracle that Anton and Poul had performed ended in tragedy nine weeks later when Poul, working down in the engine room with a sledge hammer in the stifling heat, complained of chest pains. Anton rushed him to St Stephen's Hospital in Fulham where, within twenty minutes of arriving, he had a massive heart attack. For a week he fought a desperate battle to survive. His parents and two brothers came from Denmark to be with him, but

Sleeping off New Year dinner with Anto Birkbeck in the Roaring Forties.

The *Benjamin Bowring* enters the pack-ice.

The welcoming committee at Sanae.

Old games, new surfaces. Bothie tries out the sea-ice at Sanae.

Supervising the erection of the VLF mast at Ryvingen.

Ollie engulfs a cold terrier in his wolfskin.

Poul died, aged only twenty-three, on a Saturday in July.

It was a terrible shock to everyone, especially Anton who had worked so closely with him, and a cloud lay over the expedition.

RAN: During the last few weeks everyone but Bothie worked like dogs to get things ready. Poor Bothie: for days he sensed the growing excitement and watched the non-stop packing and moving, at home as well as in the office.

Early on 2nd September 1979 Prince Charles arrived at Greenwich by helicopter wearing a black tie. He was in mourning for his uncle Earl Mountbatten, killed by an IRA bomb only four days before. For the period of court mourning he had cancelled all engagements except for the launching of the Transglobe Expedition. He had made this exception because, he said, he believed Lord Mountbatten would himself have approved the ideals of our voyage. Prince Charles, very much at home on ships, was interested in our sturdy old vessel and chatted to each of our crew. When he came to Bothie, the Prince chatted him up and scratched his back in a most friendly fashion. Whether or not he favours the Royal corgis, I never did discover, but I would not blame him for preferring Bothie.

As we moved away from Greenwich pier there was much cheering from the gathered crowds and beneath the colourful bunting in the rigging of the *Cutty Sark* a solitary bagpiper played a pibroch of farewell. Bothie lifted his nose to the summer sky and howled; whether in response to the pipes or to say his own farewell, we could only guess at. Prince Charles took the ship's wheel as far as Tilbury, then wished the team good travelling and departed by chopper.

GINNIE: Bothie and I also disembarked, for I had last minute problems to sort out with the radio equipment. In a few days I would join the land group in Paris, and we would be travelling through Europe and much of Africa in Land Rovers. I drove away from the ship in the mini with Bothie peering out from the rear window, his ears at half-mast. He was deeply hurt and bemused. His master and friends were leaving without him.

Bothie was destined to be a not entirely perfect house guest elsewhere until reunited with us in Cape Town.

RAN: The next day we disembarked the vehicles onto French soil at Dieppe and headed south. Seven long years after the day of Ginnie's idea, the Transglobe Expedition had begun.

2

Bothie Breaks the Ice

GINNIE: Hardly had the little hound begun to accept desertion by his male friends when his mistress abandoned him also. I knew it would be merely a three-month separation and that David Mason, to whose care he was entrusted, would be kind. But Bothie could know nothing except that his family had now completely gone and might never return.

RAN: David Mason, six foot four inches of ex-Guards officer, was made of extremely stern stuff. He was a full-time Transglober and the only team member whose duties lay partly in our London office, now manned by a full-time volunteer staff. He intended flying out to Cape Town to join the ship and had agreed to take Bothie with him. Meanwhile, in our absence, Bothie's behaviour was growing more and more delinquent. David thought a spot of Guards-type discipline might benefit the orphan reprobate. Battle was soon joined.

The dog did something evil and received a fair warning. David would bend down like an Indian rope trick in reverse until his Roman nose was an inch from Bothie's unrepentant black eye. Then, in a voice of low military menace, "I warn you, you little bugger, if one more cushion gets piddled on, you're for the high jump. D'you hear?"

David would then point his index finger, which must be

the longest index finger I have ever seen, at the soiled cushion (or curtain bottom or carpet) and wag it violently, all the while making a low growling sound of considerable ferocity. I feel certain that this performance, if directed at Barbara Woodhouse herself, would have turned her into a cowering jelly. But Bothie did not appear to benefit: indeed from then on whenever David, or anyone else for that matter, pointed a finger at something during the course of innocent conversation, Bothie would leap and growl viciously, with bared fangs.

Most days David worked in the barracks store-rooms. Four of us used to do the work he was now doing alone. Bothie's presence was a hindrance, but since the barracks were familiar to the dog and its other inmates all knew him, his deteriorating behaviour got him into less trouble there than it would have anywhere else.

David took a three-week holiday with friends in the Scottish Highlands. He and Bothie stayed in the lovely and ancient home of a venerable brigadier. Loveliness and venerability were lost on Bothie who set about making a dent in both. The usual trail of misplaced offerings spattered a mansion previously accustomed to centuries of house-trained gun dogs who would sooner have bruised a duck's flesh than misbehave within those dignified portals.

Not content with sullying the brigadier's property, Bothie attacked the equanimity of the brigadier's guests. One night at a dinner party a young house guest eased off her tight evening shoes during the meal. Unseen by all, Bothie slipped under the dining table and performed inside the empty shoes. At the end of dinner the girl went deathly pale and gave out a strangled cry as though something slimy had travelled down the back of her dress. For this Bothie was not forgiven nor, in that part of the Highlands, will young girls slip their shoes off at dinner for many a year. For the story soon became a favourite after-dinner tale and grew ever more colourful in the retelling.

David decided Bothie should become a confident swimmer before starting his shipboard life. But the dog showed no desire to immerse himself in water for pleasure or even for cleanliness. One day, whilst still at the brigadier's, he learnt quite by chance that he was a natural and excellent swimmer. There was a lone bothie seven miles from any habitation in the hills above the house. It was used as a stalking lodge once a year and David agreed to check out its state one weekend.

Although Bothie's stubby legs move surprisingly fast when chasing balls, he dislikes long-distance walks. Fine weather turned to rain and fog and soon the dog was soaking wet and miserable and tired. He lay down on the sodden heather to make his point but David exhorted him onwards in tones he had often used with exhausted Guardsmen. For a while Bothie responded but then they reached a long loch which barred the direct route to the bothie. David went straight to the tiny boathouse, fixed an old Seagull engine to a rickety rowing boat and hauled the craft to the lochside.

"Bothie," he yelled into the wind.

No reply. Indeed, no Bothie.

Cursing, for it was now getting dark and his lighter was the only available torch, David searched the accumulated bric-a-brac in the boathouse. Bothie was curled shivering in an old wash basin full of dirty rags.

"Good dog," David coaxed. "It's only a mile across to the hut. Better than a two mile *walk* round the loch."

Bothie's only response to this logic was a warning growl: "Leave me alone. It's dry right here."

David, wet through and aware he would be almost at the hut now but for Bothie, grabbed the tyke by his scruff and lugged him unceremoniously to the boat. Successive attempts to push the boat into the onshore wind far enough to allow the engine to be dropped and started all failed. Man and dog, lashed by wind and rain, grew tired and cross. Bothie finally revolted and dived overboard to land on a rock outcrop; he scurried back to his wash basin.

A furious David eventually had him back in the boat and at long last got the engine going at the exact moment Bothie took another dive, this time into dark, slapping wavelets. Like a born sea dog his five-inch legs clawed at the water; he ignored frequent immersions in breaking wavelets and was once more en route to his wash basin.

David gave up, beached the boat and carried Bothie (who refused to walk any further) all the way round one side of the loch to the stalker's lodge. The dog slept soundly for the next thirty-six hours, and on the way back ran well ahead of David as if to show him where the delay factor really lay.

From then on Bothie swam whenever and wherever he could.

Early in December David completed his barracks work and took Bothie to London Airport where he was put, growling but placated by a chocolate chew, in a regulation pet-box and, after being wheeled down unseen concrete byways, deposited all alone in the cavernous hold of a Boeing 727 bound for Johannesburg. David wanted Cape Town but British Airways, who sponsored all our cargo flights, did not stop there.

At the Johannesburg customs shed David asked for his dog back.

Customs officer: "Your papers."

David: "My passport, d'you mean?"

Customs officer: "Your dog papers."

David: "The dog has no papers, but I know you have

him. He was on the flight from London with me."

Customs officer: "No papers, fella, no dog."

David, who does not suffer fools or bureaucrats gladly, climbed over the customs desk, ignored the shouts of the fat gentlemen in khaki shirts and shorts who had never seen such a thing before, and stalked to the back of the shed where there were many boxes.

"Here he is," he shouted victoriously. "*This* is Bothie."

A muffled bark of joy sounded from the boxes. Fortunately a luggage tag on David's ticket stub was found to tally with a sticker on Bothie's cage and the two left the hostile customs shed together amidst much khaki muttering.

David hired a Hertz VW Beetle and drove the long dusty road south-west to the Cape. The car was soon like an oven, even with all windows open, and Bothie hated the heat. David saw few water sources all the way, but on the second day found a shallow stream beside the road. The place was crawling with yellow locusts but the water looked clean. They both drank and David let Bothie paddle and squat in the cool water. Once out, Bothie rolled on his back in the thick red dust, and crept back into the VW to have a good shake. David, his luggage and the car's interior were liberally spattered with laterite mud spots. On arrival in Cape Town David stopped at a hotel where a bottle of Sunsilk shampoo transformed the dusty scamp into a fluffy white Jack Russell groomed as though ready for Crufts.

A joyous reunion followed during which Bothie piddled all over our shoes. This took the edge off the emotion of the event for me, but Ginnie ignored it. Such is the stuff of true love.

Bothie was over two years old when he joined the ship's company, an age when dogs can be at their wickedest and most destructive. Seeing him again now, he appeared to

31

be bigger overall or at least thicker across his chest and his markings were now clearly etched. Life with David had honed an already stubborn streak into a fully fledged renegade. Anyone who could defy such Guards' discipline for three months was all set for a highly independent career.

There were sixteen crew members on the Transglobe vessel, the good ship *Benjamin Bowring*, and they came from many backgrounds and countries. All shared a desire for the voyage to succeed and each had given up a naval career for three years, unpaid, to join the expedition. Also on board were two scientists from Cape Town, a photographer and four film-makers. In all we were twenty-nine men and women, one dog and a few mice.

As we moved into our cabin on the lower deck Bothie introduced himself to those on board in order of their importance: first, Jill, the cook and the only girl member of the ship's crew. She worked in an ancient and impossibly small galley along with our rotund and good natured steward. Unlike the others, neither was ex-Navy. Jill had worked in the Patents Office in London, whilst our steward was a sort of international hippy with a biblical mane of hair. All food came from these two and Bothie had this worked out within an hour of being on board.

The bosun had shaved all his hair off and resembled a pirate. His cabin was at all times kept in a shambolic state and his clothing was stored on the floor. This, of course, provided a natural paradise for Bothie, a sort of giant double bed where he could roll about, romp and chew old slippers at will. Bothie and the bosun became great buddies.

Soon after leaving Cape Town, the last land for 2,400 miles, we set a course for the pack-ice and quickly hit storm conditions. All hands moved about ant-like, lashing and

Cold-weather sportswear.

The laden sledges of the ice group after crossing the fissured ice of the Hinge Zone.

Winter exits. But Bothie's view of what constituted outside was not the same as ours.

stacking gear, clamping hatches and taking Stugeron pills. Bothie refused to swallow his and suffered accordingly. Down in our cabin we were separated only by a single steel bulkhead from the number two hold where all the Antarctic gear was stashed. As great waves thundered over the bows the entire hull shuddered, the engines vibrated and alarming sounds issued through the cabin wall, making me wonder what vital polar items were being crushed. Each time we rolled to port, often once every two minutes, a wall of green surged past our single porthole and a thin jet of sea water shot down the cabin wall to soak the carpet.

Using lifejackets we wedged an ailing Bothie into a space between the bunks and a locker. From time to time he groaned as though the weight of the world rested on him but neither of us felt like cheering him up; our own stomachs were far from happy with the forty-seven-degree rolls hour after hour. The final straw came when a forklift truck worked loose from its lashings and toppled over, crushing a generator and spewing battery acid into the darkness of the lower hold. We left that cabin and moved to the isolated hospital cabin on the boat deck. There it was cold but quieter and less claustrophobic.

During lulls in the storm Bothie ventured all over the ship. He found the skipper's cabin by far the most palatial and approved of its soporific atmosphere – induced by the aroma of the skipper's Dunhill pipe tobacco. He left his seal of approval one morning on the skipper's doormat. This did not endear our dog to the seventy-year-old retired Admiral who was Royal Navy to his boots and liked his ships to be clean and healthy. This dislike was nurtured by a large yellow squeaking frog with bulging eyes which David Mason had given Bothie as an end of training present. He loved it and took it on ship's tours biting its squeaker to produce a high squealing noise more like an emasculated pig than any known brand of frog. The Admiral detested the sound, attempted to confiscate the frog and cast dark looks at Bothie, especially on the bridge deck which was considered semi-hallowed ground.

On Christmas Eve, after a surfeit of Black and White whisky, Anton was on bridge watch and he helped Ginnie experiment with the antiquated intercom system. This went from the bridge, direct to a tube beside the Admiral's bunk. To alert the Admiral you pulled a wire which caused the Admiral's tube to whistle piercingly. Then you simply shouted down your end of the tube. On this occasion, after waking the sleeping skipper with the whistle, they gave him a good minute of Bothie's frog on full squeak. Only the Christmas spirit prevented Bothie being throttled and his frog being thrown overboard. Perhaps the Admiral realised that even the resourceful terrier couldn't have perpetrated this latest outrage unaided.

The first officer found a special place in Bothie's heart by way of his gizzard-bag. He was on loan to us from the Royal Canadian Navy in which he was a full lieutenant. The crew called him Trapper because he resembled a grizzled old bear with full beard, wide face and small bespectacled myopic eyes. Around his waist he carried a waterproof bag which he topped up daily from Jill the cook's offal bin. Raw gizzards, chicken livers and intestines were all welcome and he chewed bits from his bag through-out the day and especially on night watches. At first Bothie shared Trapper's pickings; he had only to adopt the begging posture at the first officer's feet. But one day Trapper's pet lizard, an African gecko, disappeared from his cabin where it had roamed at will. We were all sent on a ship-wide lizard-hunt in a Force 7 gale, but the gecko was never found and Bothie received no more offal from

34

the gizzard-bag. Some months later, when Trapper left the expedition, an Indian from Bombay who ate his ice cream with Tabasco sauce was promoted to first officer, but was ignored by Bothie who didn't share his taste in food.

When the prevailing wind crossed our course at a certain latitude huge rollers would plunge by, lurching huge above the side of the gangways and occasionally bursting against the plate glass windows of the saloon. If some fool had left the saloon window ajar the sea came gushing in and surged bilge-like back and forth under the two main tables where we ate. Bothie's favourite ball games were held under these tables, watched by up to twenty semi-dazed Transglobers. His rubber balls for once needed no throwing; they moved back and forth with gravity, chased by an hysterical Bothie who, getting little or no traction on the slippery lino, would glissade quite often on his back and cannon off chair legs, impervious to anything but the nearest rubber ball.

Bothie wore a harness at all times on board which had a lead attached to it in bad conditions, just in case he were to get washed overboard, or slip on the boat deck which was the only open area. Everywhere else he was protected by the three-foot high bulwark, though the freeing ports above the scuppers were just large enough for him to be washed through in a storm. He loved to stand with his head peering through to the ocean below and barking at the waves as they bounced off the bow. But he never went near them in heavy seas and, unless strongly tethered to someone's waist, didn't go on the boat deck in rough weather. He enjoyed watching the turbulent wake as the powerful propeller ploughed through the ocean and would stand for long periods mesmerised by the bubbling water but he was always careful not to get too close to the edge. He had been sailing before in Suffolk with Anton and some friends, so we didn't have any serious worries about him jumping overboard – delinquent he may be, but he is no fool.

Anton Bowring, an avid diarist, observed:

> Bothie was a dog born into a wrong era. Were he born a century ago I feel sure that by his seventh year he would have colonised much of the world. As it was, the ship became his empire and there were few on board who could match his command. Who, after all, could involve the entire ship's company from captain to cabin boy, in searching diligently for a small well-chewed rubber ball which he himself knew perfectly well had long ago bounced overboard into the depths?

GINNIE: One evening I was throwing Bothie's bulgy-eyed frog for him on the main deck. Even more treasured than his best ball, he was thunderstruck when he saw it sailing over the top of the bulwark. Rushing back and forth along the rail he found a freeing port and peered out to see his frog floating backwards away from the ship. He barked, whined, looked pleadingly at me to *do* something. I called up to the bridge deck, "Frog overboard! Can we stop?" Venomous grins from the bridge were their own reply! Not only the Admiral was relieved to see the hideous squeaky thing bob away on the waves to a watery grave. But Bothie was distraught and returned for several days to moan pathetically through the freeing ports.

In calmer weather balls were quiescent but Bothie discovered he could throw them from the top of the companionway and they would bounce excitingly all the way down. Any sudden lurch would catapult Bothie down the steps after them and he once cut his eyelid open in a fall. What finally stopped the suicidal practice was when our

Irish radio operator, harmlessly carrying his lunch bowl of leek soup from galley to saloon, was hit by a wet rubber ball which shot off the companionway and landed in his lunch. People get unnaturally tetchy in such conditions so Bothie was forbidden the stairs for his own good.

We had a Christmas tree lashed to the mast which gale force winds tried to tear away. Christmas Day matins, carols and all, were held sitting down, any other position being unsafe. Somehow in her tiny galley Jill produced a magnificent Christmas lunch, tea and dinner, while our steward outdid himself with Irish coffees and near toxic Bloody Marys. Bothie dug into leftovers of cheese, nuts, fish, turkey, eggs, chocolate mousse and raspberry jam which he washed down with both beer and milk.

Then he went Absent Without Leave. Ran and I searched for an hour, using torches in the holds. The Scottish chief engineer and his mostly New Zealand staff swore the dog was not in their nightmarish domain. Sick with worry and soaking wet, we went back to our hospital cabin and faced the possibility he had been washed overboard.

Suddenly Ran's head shot up. "Ssssh. Listen!"

A sound as of thick bubbles bursting followed by the whine of a deflating lilo came from the clothes locker. Beneath a blue blanket and wedged upside down with his front legs in the air, Bothie was snoring in bloated post-prandial bliss. We let him be but never thereafter felt totally happy when he was out of sight for a minute.

Three days later an iceberg passed us by and soon afterwards we entered pack-ice which protected the ship from rough seas. From then on a warmly clad crewman was at all times on watch in the crow's nest advising the helmsman on open leads in the ice. When there were none we inched back and forth attempting to ram and split the less thick floes. Penguins hurried about in gaggles like late

37

commuters in black ties. Some slid down slopes on their bellies uttering joyful squawks.

Ollie took Bothie up onto the bridge deck and out on one wing to bark at the penguins. Wandering albatross winged their wide feathered spans low overhead, wheeling without effort between the masts. Orion, petrel, skua, prion and many more all crying like lost souls swooped and dived against the torn orange skies to our south.

Anton wrote:

> Bothie's territorial claims to the ship came to be understood and accepted but he seemed to assume the further right to airspace around the ship where our feathered friends glided and hovered. I often found him standing on the boat deck in great excitement, hopping from paw to paw and letting out a frantic barrage of abuse at the albatross – those same giants who in maritime history have remained so awe-inspiring that even the most hardened sailor refrains from any form of attack for fear of the consequences.

On deck the wind cut through our clothes and for the first time people began to try out polar mitts and mukluks, anoraks and balaclavas. It felt good to be doing so. A touch of Antarctic madness suddenly entered Bothie's soul at a time when at least ten of us stood silently on the bridge deck marvelling at the new world about the ship. A single staccato yap announced his presence at the entrance of the chart room. Everyone but the helmsman turned to look down at the cocky dog. There was half a broken chair leg in his mouth and with it he began a mad race in concentric circles about the bridge deck. Icebergs forgotten, everyone watched mesmerised, the same thought doubtless in every mind. Had the terrier contracted rabies?

From time to time he would throw the chair leg into the air, growling furiously, complete another lap round the Decca radar console, the helmsman at the wheel, and scowling skipper at the engine control lever, then pounce again on the bit of wood and off once more.

"Stop that, you little bugger!" It was David Mason's far from dulcet tones. "Get off the bridge at once." Surprisingly he did, chair leg and all, and the March hare act was never repeated. I smelt his breath to see if the steward had been treating him to alcohol, but the dog smelled only of cheddar cheese and was not frothing at the mouth.

"He doesn't have rabies, anyway," I reported.

"What was it then? He's never done that before."

I shrugged. "I don't know. Crossing the Antarctic Circle perhaps. Maybe the temperature change affected his brain – if he has one."

RAN: There were no more aberrations. Indeed, Bothie returned to his depressingly normal habit of relieving himself in the least suitable spots he could find. He was marking out his territory in the traditional canine way of lifting a leg all round the self-appointed boundaries. This he proceeded to do with an additional twist of his own, which was to leave more meaningful markers in every cabin to which he could gain entry, never, of course, in his own, since he knew enough not to foul his own doorstep.

No one ever caught him at it and since, in Ginnie's opinion, a dog should only be smacked when actually caught red-pawed, Bothie continued to get away with it – on Anton Bowring's door-sill, or under the desk of the ship's medic, right where he put his feet.

A particularly evil deposit was left just beside the ship's wheel during the early part of the dog watch when a man's morale is at its lowest. No light was allowed at night on the bridge, so Anton discovered the alien presence only by touch. Being a Bothie-lover and of a most long-suffering nature, Anton muttered to his co-watchkeeper: "Trying to check out our night vision, the little bastard."

Anton the diarist:

I think that Bothie tried to honour us all with his little offerings and kept to a fairly strict rota as each day he trotted off to some unsuspecting crew member's cabin. You could usually tell *where* he had been because at meal times, when we all came in from work, there was usually someone who would be looking for the dog in a determined way. To get annoyed was in fact silly, as the poor chap had not been taken into account when the ship was built some thirty years earlier and so facilities for his toilet were limited to a patch of plastic grass which we had put on the boat deck and which we all used as a sort of sun garden. For Bothie it was a dangerous area as there was little protection for him when the ship rolled (which was often) and there was always a risk that he would disappear through the guard rails and over the side of the ship.

I remember on one occasion going for a shower and being amazed to discover that Bothie had visited the bathroom. Being only a dog, albeit an intelligent one, it seemed that he had difficulty in telling the difference between the wash basin and the lavatory because, to my horror, there resting in the basin was what we on the ship called a 'floater'. The baffling thing was how he managed to get up there.

I was somewhat concerned as I had my shower because I was not too keen to remove the mysterious doings from the basin. On the other hand anyone entering the bathroom after me would be sure to think that *I* had got into a spot of bother and abused the basin myself. Who

Inside a food tunnel, where Bothie went to steal frozen eggs.

Waiting to catch a shovelful.

Digging out the supply lines.

Throwing a ball for Ginnie.

THE OLLERY

Skidoo driving lesson.

would believe me if I said it was Bothie? Perhaps I was over-reacting, but as I left the bathroom after my shower I very cautiously checked that there was no one about.

Ginnie did her utmost to put a stop to this unsavoury episode in Bothie's young life. Twice daily, when conditions allowed, she took him for long walks round and round the superstructure, up onto the fo'c's'le and back to the lifeboat deck. Every time they passed the anchor winch, a ventilator funnel, or anything remotely resembling a London lamp-post, Ginnie crooned: "Good boy, Bothie," or "Go walkies," in inviting tones. The hint was never taken, so she had to attempt a cover-up by locating the evidence before anyone else and removing it. All in all, she did quite well and bit back at anyone who complained about the ones that got away by scoffing that they were making mountains out of molehills.

On the second day of the New Year, 1980, our ice watch spotted the cliffs of Antarctica and most of those on board came on deck, some directly from their bunks with blue blankets around them. Only seven of us, including Bothie, would be dropped off and left here but for everyone it was a once-in-a-lifetime sight to be savoured in silence – black sea reflecting orange sky and a towering bastion of ice, the barrier cliffs stretched west and east as far as the eye could see.

Here was a land covered by an icecap up to three miles deep, visited by few and inhabited briefly by fewer still. Bigger in area than the whole of China plus all India, there are 760 humans living here all year round and all but a handful of these live in camps spattered around the coastal perimeter.

For many miles there was nowhere to land, just the great white ramparts hour after hour. Then the skipper and the watch officers conferred and swung close in to the cliffs. Through the glare we saw that a horseshoe bay had formed where a giant chunk of the cliff had floated away. The ice wall itself was obviously not truly Antarctica but a vast floating ice shelf still stuck to the inland ice sheet. Two further bays materialised and our skipper took us cautiously in to the third which he said was called the Polarbjorn Buchte (Polar Bear Bight). Nobody argued the point.

The great Antarctic explorer Sir Vivian Fuchs had warned us not to unload onto thin bay ice if there was an alternative. But in the Polarbjorn Buchte there was little choice; we faced either ice walls far higher than the ship's deck or the as yet unbroken sea-ice, formed the previous winter, and a mere two to three feet thick. The skipper rammed the bay ice. It seemed solid enough, so we jumped off the gunwales and hammered railway sleepers into the ice. Fist-thick ropes were lashed to these makeshift anchor points and the ship made fast.

Some South African scientists arrived from their camp sixteen miles along the coast. We had brought mail for them from Cape Town and they welcomed their new neighbours. I put on sun goggles and noticed many penguins approaching to inspect the ship. There were the Emperors, who stood waist-high, but mostly they were knee-height or less, Adélie, jackass and chinstrap. The Admiral, with less to do now we were at anchor, made friends with an outcast chinstrap. From the bridge he imitated the weird sounds he had heard other penguins utter and soon he and the chinstrap were nattering away like old friends.

Bothie stood on a lifeboat cover and stared mesmerised at the penguins and families of seal lolling in nearby melt pools. Now and again he sniffed the air as the light breeze boxed the compass, bringing with it a bewildering choice of strong new smells. He began to shiver and Ginnie took him below to don his polar gear like everyone else. The red and blue jackets both fitted snugly round his tubby post-Christmas chassis and his set of padded bootees were no problem to slip on and tape above the knee. His eye-slitted face mask caused mayhem. He hated it and used his booted front paws to force it back over his neck. Then he grabbed and shook the offending item, quickly tearing a run in the wool. After a few minutes' run around the deck he decided the bootees were a bad idea. Too cissy perhaps. So he bit the tapes off and removed the boots. We knew better than to try to make him wear a hood and boots again. He was more subtle and more determined than Houdini when it came to shrugging out of anything which constricted him. Luckily he took a liking to his polar jackets. I didn't actually catch him looking in a mirror but, by his extra swagger when dressed, I suspected he thought he cut quite a dash – Bothie of Antarctica.

Once the ship's lashings were tested and the ice against which our bows rubbed had remained unfractured for a while, one of the engineers took the jacketed Jack Russell overboard by way of a long ladder. All of him but nose, eyes and whiskers was hidden in a little rucksack he had been shoved into for his own safety. Out on the ice, a substance totally strange to him, Bothie looked about him. He was the first of his terrier race to set foot on the largest, coldest continent on earth. He yawned and licked at his paws.

3

Digging in on a Catless Continent

RAN: For the first time in the voyage Bothie found himself largely ignored as the entire crew now set to work in a race against time and weather. Over 200 tons of cargo and fuel drums were to be unloaded from the hold by hand and winched over the deck onto the ice, everything needed to see our small party through the immobility of an Antarctic winter and the attempt to reach the South Pole and cross to the other side of the continent the following year.

For four days equipment was ferried two miles inland over the bay ice by skidoos and sledges, each carrying 1,000 pounds, to an airstrip at SANAE which would be manned by Simon Grimes and Anto Birkbeck, who started to build the prefabricated hut in which they would live. On the fifth day a Southern Ocean storm crept up on us with scant warning and the walkie-talkie network between ship, skidoos and inland equipment dump buzzed with alarm.

Some drivers were stopped up at the dump but most people retired on board the ship which was soon wrenched away from its makeshift anchors by the rising sea.

The wind rose to a constant howl, slinging horizontal sleet against the *Benjamin Bowring*. The skipper hove to far enough from the ice cliffs not to be crushed between them and any southerly blown iceberg.

Great chunks of the bay were broken away and floated out to sea past the ship. We counted at least eight valuable fuel drums lost to us for ever. For some reason the Scottish chief engineer had winched his Honda motorbike onto the ice and left it there. He was much distressed when it was spotted floating towards Africa on another broken floe. Quite what a fishing skipper might think, after a good dinner with a dram or two, if he saw from his twilit bridge an ice floe floating by bearing an unmanned motorbike is difficult to imagine, but he would probably cut down on his alcohol intake.

After playing cat and mouse with us, the storm disappeared two days later. Sea and ice once again sparkled and the temperature dropped.

GINNIE: Bothie didn't seem too uncomfortable although his long terrier fur was not waterproof enough to prevent it balling up in the freezing wet conditions. Ever burgeoning globules of ice hung from his stomach and the fur over his paws tinkled together when he moved. His eyelashes, and Bothie has long dark Latin-lover lashes, slowly glued together where sets of mini-iceballs formed at the tips, clanking like castanets as he blinked.

Because his failed attempts to instigate a ball game were having a demoralising effect on him, he decided to amuse himself. He vanished from the bridge where I was on radio watch. After a while I thought I had better look for the little horror to be sure he wasn't doing some damage. On entering the door to the duty mess there was a low gurgling growl. Bothie was on the bench hiding under the table, devouring a large lump of butter, his nose now a greasy yellow mess, his black eyes flashing as I tried to get to him. Nothing was going to stop him, and maybe he knew that his daily intake of fat – like our own – should be increased. I left him to it and hoped he wouldn't be sick later.

Later that day a barrage of yapping erupted which pene-trated the radio earphones. I dashed outside frightened he had jumped overboard but found he had persuaded someone to carry him ashore and our hero was face to face with a ferocious Adélie penguin. Whether it was the penguin or Bothie who was at bay could not be ascertained, since they were both in the middle of a flat white expanse. Goodness knows what the penguin was doing so far from its friends, but it had strayed onto Bothie's self-claimed territory and, at first glance, looked like a fairly insubstantial foe. No sooner had the brave terrier, forgetting his lessons with the London cats, committed himself to a full frontal attack, than the evil-smelling bird puffed itself up, arched its neck and spread out stubby flightless wings. At least four inches taller than Bothie, with a beak capable of causing damage, the Adélie was no longer an attractive target.

Bothie is no fool and, realising his error of judgement, obviously intended to break off the engagement. He turned and saw several of us watching him. Pride prevented outright retreat, so he made a further imprudent sally at the odoriferous squawking apparition, but his legs skidded on the wet ice. The penguin, hissing like an angry goose, darted forward to take advantage of the terrier's mishap, but Bothie recovered just in time and, audience or no, fled to join the crowd of ship's crew, now no longer working, but laughing at the expense of our hero's lost dignity; he took no heed of their taunts of "Penguin, Bothie – kill the penguin!" and took off to the stern of the ship with ears and tail lowered.

The unloading was completed without further kit losses and the ship made ready to escape before the pack-ice could close in and crush her, as had been the fate of Shackleton's *Endurance* some sixty years ago. It was sad

46

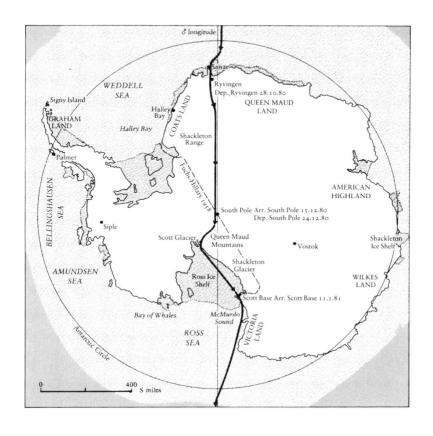

Within the map:

δ longitude

WEDDELL
SEA

Sanae

Ryvingen
Dep., Ryvingen 28.10.80

QUEEN MAUD
LAND

Signy Island

GRAHAM
LAND

Halley
Bay

COATS LAND

Halley Bay

Shackleton
Range

Palmer

Fuchs-Hillary 1958

AMERICAN
HIGHLAND

BELLINGSHAUSEN
SEA

Siple

South Pole Arr. South Pole 15.12.80
Dep. South Pole 24.12.80

Vostok

Shackleton
Ice Shelf

Scott Glacier

Queen Maud
Mountains

Shackleton
Glacier

WILKES
LAND

AMUNDSEN
SEA

Ross Ice
Shelf

Scott Base Arr. Scott Base 11.1.81

Bay of Whales

McMurdo
Sound

VICTORIA LAND

ROSS
SEA

Antarctic Circle

0   400
          S miles

ANTARCTICA

47

when our friends sailed away and disappeared beyond the cliffs of Polarbjorn Buchte. We would not see them or our floating home for a year, perhaps two.

RAN: The Twin Otter ski-plane piloted by Giles, with Gerry his engineer, had arrived after a hazardous fifteen-day flight from England. In Brazil they'd eaten a Christmas lunch of piranha and chips. Now they had three short weeks to move some 108,000 pounds of cargo one stage further from our coastal dump to Ryvingen, a point 300 miles inland at 6,000 feet above sea level which was to be our winter base on the southern rim of the Borga massif, the last feature of any sort for 1,400 miles to the South Pole. Our two-man hut-building team of Simon and Anto had finished building their own hut by the airstrip and were dropped off with Ryvingen's prefabricated cardboard hut sections, shovels and spanners, to begin constructing our camp.

The ice group of Charlie, Ollie and myself now set out with our skidoos on the first stage of a polar crossing of over 2,000 miles. Our route passed through a fault called the Hinge Zone that was rotten with fissured ice and an early test of both men and equipment.

GINNIE: Until the loads were ferried inland, Bothie, Giles, Gerry and I remained based at the SANAE dump in a tiny hut on stilts, all of eight feet square. Bothie disliked the hut almost as much as the bitter conditions outside. It was not at all what I had expected as, although it was not very cold, there was usually a wind blowing. The blown snow would melt on contact with whatever it fell on – the hut, fuel drums, and all the supplies waiting to go up to Ryvingen. Huge, weird-shaped ice formations were created and stuck firmly to all these items, human and canine too, if they were foolish enough to go out. Even a brief exit to collect snow for water, or to answer the calls of

Boing . . .boing . . .boing time.

In the rubbish box after supper.

The ball-in-a-sock-in-a-sock-in-a-boot game.

nature would result in becoming wet and clogged by the cloying muck. One morning Bothie came back into the hut looking more miserable than usual and limping. He had caught his foot in the metal boot scraper outside the door and wrenched a claw. He licked at it all day and refused to allow Gerry or me near, but we could see it was not healthy. That evening when he fell asleep we did our best using the First Aid tin but the following morning it was worse. He soon tore away the lint bandage and began to lick the now inflamed paw and so, apart from cosseting the wretched little hound, there was very little else one could do for him.

Bad weather days, mist and snow were on the increase with approaching winter. Giles was racing against time to ferry the last equipment up to Ryvingen, aware that he and Gerry must leave Antarctica and get the long South Atlantic flights behind them before the vicious winter storms began. Bothie's paw was still causing him a lot of misery. He would whimper quietly as he licked it and moaned if I held it even gently in my hand. I had never known him so unhappy and became quite alarmed at the prospect that was facing us. However, the ice group were making good progress, so the time had come for Bothie and me to say goodbye to Gerry and move up to Ryvingen ourselves.

Quite unexpectedly Bothie seemed to like the look of this new adventure and stood wagging his tail with some enthusiasm. We climbed aboard the Twin Otter, jammed to the gunwales with cargo, and perched on a forty-five-gallon fuel drum until Giles invited us to join him in the cockpit. This was much more fun and Bothie took to flying like a duckling to water. Sitting on my knee he watched Giles with great interest and respect as he made all the pre-flight checks. Then we were off. I held my hands over the dog's ears to save them from the hideous roar as Giles used the thrust of one engine to turn us around to face into the wind for the take-off. We raced down the strip and in a flash were airborne. Soaring up over sea-ice and the great white cliffs which formed the little bay where we had unloaded the equipment, we turned and then headed inland. Bothie shook himself free of my clutches and tried to stand on my knees, forgetting his foot was still sore, making it clear he wanted to see what was happening. I held his fat little body so he could rest his good front paw on the dashboard and peer out of the window along the short stubby nose of the aircraft. He was riveted by the view and stayed glued to the windscreen as we climbed higher and higher up over never ending mountains and massive expanses of nothingness. It was magnificent and nothing was lost on Bothie, he was enjoying it every bit as much as I was.

"It is truly God's country, isn't it," Giles said over the crackling headphones. I could understand what he meant and why he felt so happy flying here, free as the wildest bird and master of his own destiny. He was completely in his element and totally relaxed.

We arrived over Ryvingen Mountain after a two-hour spectacular and saw the long lines of equipment and the three huts that were already up. Simon and Anto met us with skidoos and empty sledges to take the equipment we had on board. Bothie, forgetting his sore foot, rolled and tumbled in the soft powdery snow like a new born lamb. It was wonderful to be there at last and the sun was shining. There was not a cloud in the sky. It was considerably colder and drier and the effort of walking or working soon made one tired.

Bothie also was affected by the altitude for a day or two, but he was too excited to miss anything. He visited every hut, every box in the equipment lines, every flagpole and every shovel in the snow, and marked his territory with precision. This was his new home. Then Anto mixed him a bowl of Chum and biscuits and he collapsed on a blanket by the fire and slept. The paw seemed to heal almost overnight and although the claw was still loose, it was not going to stop his activities. He had much to do and much to investigate.

The next few days saw the completion of the huts, radio masts erected, antennae hung, and a never-ending supply of boxes stowed. One morning whilst we were having a well earned cup of coffee, Simon and Anto called out in unison to Bothie to shut up. He had been barking incessantly for five minutes and not, we thought, at anything in particular. But we were wrong. He ignored their rebuke and continued to bark. Fifteen minutes later we saw three black dots to the north. After a tortuous overland journey through a maze of black mountains and unnamed nunataks, the three-man ice group had made it. We lit a flare and Bothie increased his volume.

As they came nearer there was no holding Bothie who took off to greet the new arrivals, four stubby legs disappearing downhill in a cloud of soft snow. On reaching Ran's skidoo he tried to stop but did a somersault, continuing on past Charlie and past Ollie at the rear, before wheeling round to race back uphill, still yapping a frenzied greeting, and lead them into camp. Somebody threw a snowball for Bothie who retrieved a mouthful of it before guiding them into the main hut where we would sleep, eat, work and play for the next nine months, and showing them the area he had staked out for himself behind the heater.

Soon Simon and Anto departed for the coastal dump where they would spend the long winter a few miles from the South African scientists, and Giles made his last flight up with cargo and Gerry. Whilst unloading the last few items Bothie discovered that Gerry was a cricketer and really knew how to throw a ball. But his delight was short-lived as Gerry climbed into the Twin Otter with Giles and took off. After a last low pass over the camp they roared away to the west, waggling their wings and disappearing from view behind the mountains. Five fur-clad creatures stood silently for a minute gazing into the empty sky, alone in a snowy silent wilderness – 1,400 miles to our south, the South Pole, 300 miles to our north, the nearest human beings, Simon and Anto and the South Africans. But we knew that whatever happened during the next nine months there was no way of getting help. We could only rely on our own wits to survive. In a month the sun would disappear and stay away for the long dark winter. By then we must have a self-contained fortress ready in which to survive hurricane-force winds and a wind-chill factor, or absolute temperature, which would plunge well below −80°C.

Bothie gave a small bark and fetched his ball where it had been left by Gerry and dropped it at Ran's feet. Ran threw the ball down the hill and said, "Well, we'd better get started."

4

Bothie of the Antarctic

RAN: Fire was our single greatest fear, for we burned volatile fuels in our heaters, so it was important to have a quick exit from each hut. As the doors were soon made useless by mounting snow, I decided to dig tunnels directly from the doorways. In three weeks of digging and shovelling I fashioned a system of tunnels 200 yards long and seven foot high. Wide enough to store every item we possessed, they also housed a thirty-foot slop pit, a lavatory alcove and a ready repairs room. Bothie was some help in that he prevented me going round the twist with the sheer monotony of endless hours shifting tons of snow. His antics attacking the flying shovel-loads, the wrongly-timed leaps and somersaults which ended with his missing the lip of the trench and flying down to join me seven feet below, all helped to keep me distracted.

When he tired of chase-the-shovel-load, he would often switch to fight-the-iceball, which consisted of finding a football-sized chunk of hardened snow, almost ice, and attacking it with the apparent intention of eating it bit by bit. Wrapping his front paws around the iceball he would wrestle, rolling and kicking, all the while talking to himself in frustrated squeaky whimpers. Breaking away at the end of a round he would dash about in circular forays, glissading on hard ice patches and tumbling head over heels in sudden drifts of soft snow. When tiring of the inanimate snow chunk he would quickly look around to see if Ollie, Charlie or Ginnie were to be found, but they were busy inside their respective huts – so back to the tunnel digging for more shovel-flying.

We didn't know a great deal about the nature of crevasses and their most likely locations but, after a cursory examination of the immediate camp surrounds, decided Bothie could safely wander at will, providing the weather was settled. The same went for the rest of us. We could ill afford injuries, since for nine months there would be no outside medical aid available, and it seemed a sound idea to avoid Ollie's ministrations if humanly possible. Ollie had been on a course for three weeks and, among other useful teachings, had observed nine appendix operations which in theory meant he could remove ours. For a week or so after the course he had been itching to get at an appendix, but a year later I seriously wondered if he could remember which side of the stomach to cut open. His dental course had only lasted three days, and he'd not had time to become a vet.

GINNIE: One day I was ski-ing down to check the eighty-foot radio mast we had erected on arrival. As usual Bothie ranged around, hunting for non-existent scents between bouts with his football which he pushed across the snow. Ran was digging fuel drums out of a drift at the time and heard my scream on the wind.

"Bothie, Bothie! Come here!" But he was upwind of me and it was impossible to hear each other when the wind blew around the camp. The cause of my alarm was soon obvious to Ran as I gesticulated wildly at a great brown bird, which appeared to be the size of a heron, swooping down low over the blurred shape of Bothie who was now racing after a snow scurry.

RAN: The primordial background of black crag, blue ice wall and spiralling snow-devils sweeping the huge empty plateau made me think of pterodactyls and giant rocs. I dropped my shovel and tried to run but it was hopeless through the drifts. We had no weapons in Antarctica, since there were no predators in all the continent for us to fear.

Bothie must have sensed the danger, or perhaps its shadow flitting over the snow. He fled straight for Ginnie, his powerful legs pumping piston-like over drifts and sastrugi ice ridges. Ginnie's proximity probably saved him, since the bird was quite clearly bent on attacking. Ginnie waved her arms wildly and the brute swerved and flew up into the air.

"A Southern skua," murmured Ollie, our amateur ornithologist, as he patted Bothie. "Nasty habits and nastier beak."

GINNIE: After the skua scare we *made* Bothie wear his red waistcoat more often on the principle that skuas do not attack waistcoat-wearing creatures. But after a few days we decided there were no further signs of life except ourselves. Indeed we saw nothing else for ten months except a fly that had been hiding in a packing box. It flew around in the hut for two days and was found feet-up in Bothie's bed.

Autumn turned to winter which as far as we were concerned meant that even at midday, there was no glimpse of the sun. Long lines of cord between bamboo poles were our only guide from hut to hut especially during those weeks when the moon disappeared and the wind tore shrieking through the half buried camp.

RAN: Ollie was involved in a daily meteorological programme and often the needle of his electric anemometer would lurch from zero to an instant sixty, seventy, even eighty knots and, as it did so, a roar like a locomotive in a tunnel would pass over the hut. Caught outside by the sudden katabatic gusts, we were more than once knocked clean off our feet and deposited on our backs in the snow.

What did we do for all those months of darkness with no TV, no office, no outsiders and all that forced togetherness? Certainly there was no boredom. Ollie has said in many ways it was one of the happiest periods of his life. I think we avoided serious strife simply by *not* being together, except for two meals a day and chance meetings up the food tunnel or down along a safety line in the moonlight. We were all kept busy twelve hours a day, often more. Each of us had an area of responsibility that the others counted upon but seldom interfered with. Only Bothie strayed across the lines of demarcation and was welcome. He made it his daily business to check on each of the denizens of Ryvingen and soon worked out the best time of day or night to pay his visits.

GINNIE: We called it day but in reality it had become twenty-four hours of darkness, sometimes lit by the moon, sometimes by the flickering green of Aurora Australis, with breakfast by electric light at one end and supper the same way at the other. Since everyone liked Bothie's visits, he was cosseted and fed in each hut. After breakfast in Ollie and Charlie's end of the main living hut he would take his leave of Charlie, who did the cooking, and run down the long tunnels to the furthest exit ramp, pushing his way through the tarpaulins which kept out the light snow.

Following Ollie's scent in the snow the terrier jumped down two feet through a hollowed-out fuel drum and nosed along a corkscrew ice-lined shaft that ended at a plywood door. If this was shut, he scratched at it till Ollie let him in. Everything in the generator hut was always spick and span for that was Ollie's way, but the hut was

Bi-monthly bath time is imminent and unavoidable.

Putting on the agony.

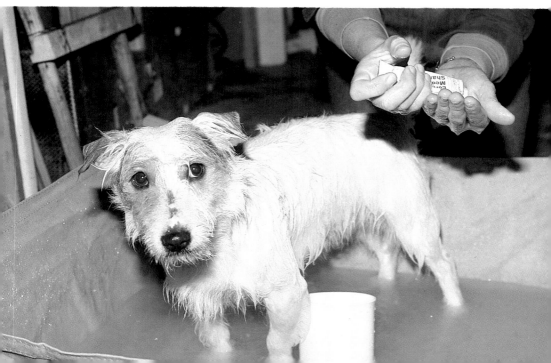

Ducking for balls in the monthly wash is good entertainment.

To scold him you had to catch him.

Exhaustion and peace.

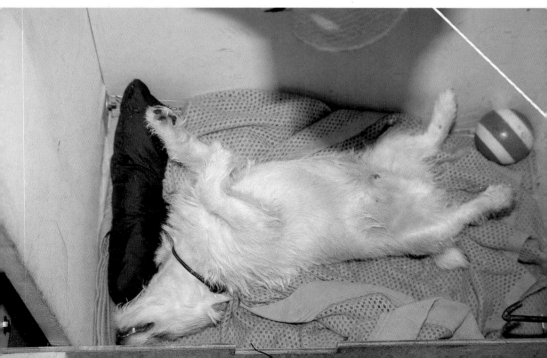

Can Ollie really be reading *The Hobbit* for the fourth time?

pervaded with a blend of smells which fascinated Bothie, a heady mix of fish oils and grease, diesel and tobacco, for Ollie, like the rest of us, smoked far too many cigarettes. His garage visits usually resulted in his fur becoming streaked with black oil as he clambered over and through the generator Ollie was servicing at the time, but his help invariably earned him a Marathon chocolate bar. Charlie rationed us to a Mars, a Marathon and another slab of milk chocolate per day. Ollie liked the Marathon least and a touching daily ritual took place as Bothie sat patiently, anticipation driving his tail to a frenzy of motion, as Ollie slowly unwrapped the nutty bar.

From Ollie's power kingdom, licking his chops at the last particles of the Marathon bar, Bothie's next port of call was usually downhill to the radio hut some 150 yards away along another safety line. Maybe he was unaware of the rope itself, but his nose took him unerringly along the line of wooden poles that carried it, and he refreshed his scent at each post. I would have received a call from Ollie on the VHF walkie-talkie to tell me the hound had left and was on his way, so I'd keep an ear open for his scratch at the door. Sliding down the rounded ice-steps he'd negotiate the coaxial cables which entered the porch from various radio masts, and clamber over heaps of newly drifted snow which blasted through tiny holes in the porch cover as stubbornly as it was cleared away. Yapping loudly at the door – for he had learnt that mere scratching did not always penetrate the electronic orchestra of my world – Bothie would gain admittance.

He seemed to like the radio hut and its cacophony of noise, although I couldn't understand why. Sometimes it would pierce the eardrums as loud screams and nerve-shattering crackle and hiss reverberated around the walls. What he enjoyed most was when there was a storm blowing outside and the built up static in the coaxial cables would seek an earth. Because the camp was built on deep snow, some mile thick, and the temperature was so low, there was no real earth. With the lights in the hut turned off, it was great fun to watch the electricity flicker along the metal foil surface of the hut lining, creating a blue and yellow light that darted in all directions. Bothie would sit for long periods trying to follow it on its weird route around the hut walls and ceiling. I had built him a cosy bed of an old duvet jacket and a Brentford nylon blanket between one wall and the kerosene heater. Biscuits and dog chews were ready at all times and sometimes a hoarded Mars bar, the sine qua non of Bothie's existence.

Since he expected this daily treat by way of a reward for making the trip so far, he would try to stop me getting on with my work until he got his way. As with most terriers, the begging position is natural and easy for Bothie and maintainable for as long as the stubbornness of the current victim makes it necessary. His system was the good old keep-it-up-long-enough-and-they'll-give-in tactic – roll your eyes, winge in a pathetic B-flat once every five seconds and intersperse the occasional belch to stress your message. It's really just a form of simplified hypnosis. RAN: When, inevitably, the Mars bar paper crackled and the hand stretched across bearing the four-inch piece of paradise, Bothie's face became a study in bliss, in sheer unadulterated pleasure. Closing his eyes and quivering his wet nostrils, he licked the cold chocolate coating with a delicate caress of his small pink tongue. Then as the gourmand took over from the gourmet, his little bouche became a gueule and his essen became fressen. After this werewolf transformation took place, to put a hand anywhere near the dog was to invite a bout of quite unBothie snarling.

Once the chocolate had disappeared, Bothie invariably stood up and licked the donor's hand to show his gratitude and double check for any remaining traces. Then, within minutes, he would be nestling in his four-star bed. By midday when I came down to refill the fuel tank from a drum outside Ginnie's hut, the terrier would be snoring with his upper lip curled back and all four legs in the air, and I'd know he had had his daily treat from Ginnie's larder.

GINNIE: During the latter half of the long darkness I worked at the Very Low Frequency research hut that was by necessity quarter of a mile from the main camp and up a long slope to the east. We also kept emergency equipment stored there, food, fuel, a small generator, medical supplies, clothing etc., in case for any reason the main camp was destroyed.

Bothie maintained a bed and visitor's status there too, but it was his least favourite haunt. He was uneasy, but then so was I. From time to time through the winter, while following the long line of bamboos through the dark or moonlit spaces, I thought I heard footsteps behind me and a gentle whistling. At times there was a strong 'presence' but not a frightening or unpleasant one. Poor Bothie had his own personal ghost problem.

RAN: As the variety of different sounds he was accustomed to identify had become very narrow in our winter world, Bothie got edgy when strange sounds did occasionally startle him. On afternoons when moonlight and rare settled conditions permitted, Charlie and Ollie donned heavy clothes and langlauf skis. Half a mile east of the camp Ryvingen Mountain soared its massive flank into the darkness below the slow revolving seahorse of Scorpio. Bothie went with the skiers if he was in the mood for exercise and they would take one of his rubber balls along.

BOTHIE THE POLAR DOG

One evening Ollie led the other two to a part of the mountain where a spectacular wind scoop was hollowed amphitheatre-like beneath a spur of rock. The sound effects caused by this natural bowl were unexpected and, to Bothie, inexplicable.

Approaching the darkened rocks, the terrier was spooked and barked defensively into the gloom ahead. To his amazement the gloom barked back, not once but several times with a weird hollow cadence, quite unlike that of any dog he had ever known.

Now Bothie had made up his mind months ago that there were no other dogs in this part of the world. He, Bothie, was top dog in the Antarctic. He was sure of it. So as the horrible demon-dog noise echoed slowly away, the terrified terrier fled, tail clamped down, five-inch legs pounding the snow, straight for the main tunnel and the safety of Ginnie's lap, shaking and whimpering.

That evening he ate nothing but paced the hut growling and constantly alert. The slightest outside sound had him out of his bed, teeth bared and ears cocked. For a whole week he ate little, kept to the main hut and continued to search for the devil-dog with the dreadful voice. Then Ollie coaxed him out for another ski trip and he saw there was nothing lurking in or beyond the tunnels. Slowly he forgot his fears.

Some days the wind came from longitude 110° and would blow right through the camp, whipping the snow from the high inland spaces of the plateau horizontally through the darkness. Even with goggles and a heavy parka it was often necessary to walk backwards up the safety line and clip onto it with a rope attached to the waist. It was hard not to be blown off your feet, or to stumble over the newly formed sastrugi but, if you did, at least you were still in touch with the safety line.

GINNIE: At Bothie's height above ground level such conditions were impossible and one or two nasty experiences had taught him the uselessness of struggling against the elements. One morning after spending eleven hours in the research hut, we tried to get back to the main hut, but the wind was so fierce that I could hardly get the lid off the escape hatch. Bothie had to travel inside my parka, zipped up to the neck, and struggling frantically as I fell over. That experience taught him the foolishness of visiting the hut of weird noises, where you only got a headache from the fumes of the little naphtha heater.

To decide whether to make a trip outside he would go to the end of the main tunnel and push his nose under the tarpaulin. If conditions looked reasonable he'd go, but otherwise he would turn back. Sometimes he didn't even bother to do this, as the walls in the hut shook and the tiny frozen ice particles battered the cardboard roof. Then he would curl up in his bed and feign sleep, peeping out of one eye as the door opened to check who the fool was leaving the safety of the hut.

Sitting out a storm presented Bothie with the problem of where to go and do what a dog's got to do. His sanitary arrangements bothered the rest of us more than they ever bothered him. 'Outside' to Bothie meant anywhere beyond the hut door, not all the way to the furthest tunnel exit. Inside our long winding storage tunnels Ran had cut a narrow central walkway and Bothie liked to think of this as a road with low walls each side, cocking a leg occasionally to ensure his safe return journey. This irritated Ran, since not only had he dug the tunnels but he had to keep the walkway clean and safe. But despite months of carrying him by his scruff, growling furiously, to the exit, and meaningful pointing, David Mason-style, Bothie stubbornly continued to foul Ran's beautifully sculptured ice tunnels. In the end we just had to admit defeat on that one.

RAN: Being cooped up together for nine months inevitably placed a strain on personal relationships and every now and again this burst to the surface in minor remarks tinged with vitriol. Bothie's presence was a strong factor in relieving tensions. Awkward silences and explosive atmospheres were often punctured by a comic whimper or the way he demanded a ball thrower, or even his reprehensible habit of clamping himself to Ollie's trouser leg at supper times as Ollie tried to walk about the room. It was always Ollie's leg for no good reason that we could think of.

"You randy little devil. Get off!" from an indignant Ollie.

"Go on, give it him, Bothie. You show him!" from Charlie.

GINNIE: In an instant petty differences would fall into perspective and hurt feelings fade away as all four of us were helpless with giggles which only seemed to encourage the clinging terrier. Having him to pet and throw balls for, to scold or mutter sweet nothings to, was in itself worth a dozen paperback books.

Every evening after supper, except during the worst blizzards when our schedule went awry fighting encroaching drifts, or when the wind-chill factor reached −84°C, Ollie would leave, torch in hand, and walk to the generator hut, often taking Bothie with him. When he got there he would flick the main power switch on and off once or twice; this would flash the lights all over camp, giving warning that torches or candles were needed within two minutes. Then with a final flick all power ceased and the noise of the generator faded away, leaving only the sounds of nature. After blocking up the exhaust holes and pulling a tarpaulin over the generator tunnel entrance the two returned to the living hut. The same procedure in reverse brought the camp to life again each morning – but Ollie usually had to drag Bothie growling sleepily out by the scruff of his neck as he did love his bed.

At night, Charlie, Ran and I often sat round a candle and, using matchsticks in lieu of immense sums of money, we would play cards or one of our many board games. Ollie was usually tired because his six-hourly meteorological forays in all weathers woke him at midnight, so he would lie above us in his bunk reading.

We gamblers needed to concentrate because games sparked an unspoken degree of competitive spirit between us. Bothie did not appreciate this and invariably produced a rubber ball. Various methods developed to keep the pest at bay – a ball inside a sock, inside a sock, inside a boot, inside a clothes box was one solution it took him several minutes to unravel. He soon tired of the silly idea of us putting on his outdoor jacket and pushing the ball inside the jacket on his back. His favourite was the dustbin game.

Under the sink was a big cardboard box holding the rubbish bag. This was always emptied straight after supper with the slops and so in the evening we took to throwing Bothie's ball in it. He leapt in, then, like a jack-in-the-box, out again plus ball. Three dozen leaps later Bothie was panting. Eight dozen leaps later he was whacked and climbing out of the box was a huge effort. After some forty minutes he was usually asleep, ball in mouth, deep inside the box, having failed to climb out that last time. We could then concentrate on our game and a long suffering Ollie could go to sleep.

We tried our best to find Bothie's toys when he lost them, but his carelessness slowly whittled away the ball and bone supply. Chews were all gone after five months and sadly a strong wind from the north somehow found his only rubber football and blew it away. Unless it fell down a crevasse, it may well have reached the far side of Antarctica by now.

Midwinter arrived, 21st June. In Antarctica it is celebrated like Christmas as December of course falls in the high peak of summer activity. But from 21st June the nights were getting shorter. It was a promise that the sun would return. Everyone contributed something to the five stockings hanging up in the kitchen that morning and Bothie helped to unwrap the strangest assortment of gifts that could have ever been left by Santa Claus. Using old socks, stuffed with rags or shirt tails sewn up and filled with paper, bits of foam mattress or cardboard, I made the toyless terrier little legless men to chew and shake in terrier fashion. They were soon destroyed and left in a million pieces scattered around the hut. He would bring the last soggy remnant to me as an offering – or an advice note that he needed another.

RAN: Improving weather encouraged exploration further afield. We knew of a long deserted hut some eleven miles from Ryvingen which had been erected some years before by an expedition of South African and Norwegian scientists who abandoned it when it began to cave in.

"They must have left some goodies when they went," Charlie maintained.

"All stale by now probably," said Ollie.

"Not at this temperature. And even in summer their old hut will be out of the sun. It fact it must be several feet under the snow by now." Charlie was adamant, so we decided to find the buried camp and whatever treasures it held.

"We can't leave Ginnie by herself here," said the everthoughtful Ollie.

"Why not?" joked Charlie. "She'll be alone long enough when we set out for the Pole."

Ryvingen at twilight.

Bothie yearning round the generator for a Mars Bar.

Fiddling on the roof.

Bothie and Ginnie sulked convincingly, so it was agreed they could use a spare skidoo and Bothie could travel in a rucksack. We took a tent in case of trouble. The weather stayed clear and we came upon a radio mast where once the camp had bustled. But despite digging exploratory shafts in several places, there was no sign of the base hut, so we left empty-handed. Bothie, after his first true polar foray, had a frost-nipped ear and a sore eye but, as always, new activities roused his spirits and he was unbearably chirpy for days afterwards.

Later Charlie and I went back and did find an entry tunnel to the base hut. We brought back badly needed nails to shore up our own tunnel roofs, plus a goodly supply of ten-year-old groceries. Some, like the tins of brussels sprouts, were inedible.

GINNIE: Despite our new supplies, Charlie had to ration foodstuffs with care and nobody could steal from the food tunnels without his go-ahead. This unspoken law was obeyed by all except Bothie.

Our eggs were by now eight or nine months old and, although frozen for much of that time, they had been through the tropics. They tasted extremely odd, to put it mildly, and looked even odder when broken into a frying pan. But if you eat an egg every day for six months and the addled state increases imperceptibly over that period, you get used to it by stages and weaned gradually off good onto bad eggs. Giles and Gerry, in contrast, were both very ill at the mere smell of the eggs when they returned after nine months. Bothie was addicted to these frozen addled eggs and, however hard Charlie tried to hide his egg store in the food tunnels, Bothie quickly outwitted him and stole an egg a day, sometimes more.

When nobody was about he would bring his daily egg into his warm bed and peel the shell from the frozen contents. Then he would lick the addled frozen mess like a lollipop until he reached the yolk – a hard but manageable golf-ball of orange. This he would roll around in his mouth like a connoisseur before a bite and a gulp disposed of the delicacy, leaving only the shell as evidence of his misdemeanour to be hidden under his blanket. If caught red-handed, the usual fierce take-it-if-you-dare growling and flashing eyes routine was performed. But the worst of it all was in the evenings when Bothie let loose sulphurous egg gases, overpowering anyone in the neighbourhood, especially Ollie whose bed-space was immediately above Bothie's.

Bothie's bed was also full of old bones, since our leftovers all went to him and there was no room for him to eat except outside or in his bed. He liked having bones in his sleeping quarters anyway; it gave him a sense of security and they had all been carefully 'buried'. Charlie kept frozen joints in his tunnel, including racks of lamb. To make them more manageable he brought chunks inside and applied a Black and Decker saw to them on the kitchen table. Bothie would sit under the table catching the frozen saw-dust as it settled.

Inside the cardboard huts our furniture was mostly made out of cardboard packing cases. Personal clothing and boots were kept in lidless boxes stacked sideways. Possibly because of sharp bones digging into him in his own bedspace Bothie took to burrowing cosy nests among sweaters and socks inside our box shelves. Charlie and Ollie turned a blind eye to this at first but their patience wore thin. One morning poor Charlie discovered a neat mound on one boot. He gave me an enraged shout. Apologising profusely, I removed the frozen offering and cleaned the boot as best I could. He put it on and then the other. An awful pallor suffused his normally ruddy visage.

"My God," he breathed, "he's pee'd *in* this one!" For a while Charlie was speechless. Then, quietly, he hissed "That's *it*! No more. He goes up your end from now on. He's your dog, he can sleep in and foul your end of the hut!"

There was no answer to this; indeed I was amazed that Charlie and Ollie had been so long suffering and stuck it out for two thirds of the winter. The incident was not mentioned again but to this day I haven't worked out why Bothie was so stupid, for he must have known he couldn't get away with it.

I made a new bed for the disgraced terrier under our own plank-bed and raised all our clothing, boots and valuables well above ground level.

RAN: Because we spent most of the time in separate huts and because of the conditions outside, small errors could have serious consequences. During the seventh month of our incarceration there were some alarming moments. The slightest lack of forethought was often later regretted. One morning Ginnie returned for breakfast after a night at the research hut. Outside the wind-chill factor was −90°C. Checking the cause of a burning sensation on her leg, she discovered her metal Zippo lighter in her trouser pocket had burnt through to the skin in a single patch the exact shape of the lighter. Another day I called her on the walkie-talkie, a normal safety precaution in bad weather, but there was no reply, so I pushed my way against the wall of wind outside and found her staggering about the radio hut, all but overcome by carbon monoxide fumes from a portable generator charging batteries in the porch area. Ollie had suffered similar experiences but fortunately recognised the symptoms and rushed out into the fresh air before it was too late. There were panics, too, with battery acid, with petrol in the eye, with petrol instead of kerosene in the radio hut stove, static electricity shocks from the antenna, as well as back and stomach troubles. But luckily, by the beginning of the end of the long winter, nothing had seriously damaged any of us and Bothie had survived better than all of us.

One noon the sun returned to Antarctica. We had become used to living without sunlight, but there was nonetheless a sense of elation when Ollie shouted, "Here she comes. What a beautiful sight!"

We ran down the tunnels and caught the briefest glimpse of the sun's upper rim as it slid across the bloodred horizon. Each day there were longer periods of twilight outside the true sun hours and we used the time fully in preparation for the coming journey. Increasingly I felt a pit in my stomach when I thought of what lay ahead. The Antarctic experts in the USA and New Zealand had warned us there was no way we could cross the continent using skidoos. Who were we to question their opinion? After all we had no experience of the vastness of the high inland plateau that lay to our immediate south, 2,000 miles of it.

As the day of departure approached the atmosphere about the camp altered. People were quieter, more wrapped up in their thoughts. Bothie seldom slept as was his wont with his eyes squeezed tight, dead to the world. Now he was loath to close his eyes at all unless everyone was in bed. He seemed to fear we might get up to something he might miss unless he kept alert. He knew there was something in the wind.

Early on 28th October with the thermometer at −50°C, and a steady twenty-knot wind, we said goodbye to Ginnie and Bothie and headed south into a great white valley, the terrier's bark ringing in our ears. In a few hours we passed by a lone rock nunatak named Stignaben, the last feature

on earth for 1,400 miles to the South Pole. We were in
unmapped terrain where no human being had trod since
the beginning of time.

5

Forbidden Dog at the South Pole

GINNIE: The three men had long since disappeared from sight when Bothie joined me in the radio hut. I was trying to bury my fears in activity. I managed, with difficulty, to make contact with RAE Farnborough, over 8,000 miles away, where the ever dependable and reassuring voices of our UK radio base operators passed me the day's news from home, mostly good luck messages from our families, sponsors and well-wishers. The frequency began to fade but not before they received my report that the attempt to cross Antarctica had begun. Sitting on a stool in front of the now hissing receiver, I gathered Bothie up in my arms, gave him a cuddle, and found myself talking to him as much to ease my own sadness as his.

For three days Bothie moped, only moving from one bed to another in the various huts, depending on where I went. He refused to eat. Even the lure of a Mars or Marathon would not shake him out of his despondency. As far as he was concerned, he might never again see those good friends who took him ski-ing; even the rebellious joy of growling at a furious master on the discovery of some new misdemeanour was gone perhaps forever.

For my own part, three people had now become dependent on my dubious skills with the radio and antennae for an immediate response should there be any problems or an accident. This involved between sixteen and eighteen hours a day just listening on the radio for their call in case it came. Only when they were safe in the tent at night and had given me their position, could I relax and take Bothie with me on the daily round of the extensive antenna farm which I had developed. With communications to the ice group, England, other bases in Antarctica, and the aircraft all to be maintained, the area to be visually checked was probably a square mile and Bothie soon learnt to accept this as his only daily accompanied exercise.

Giles and Gerry once again made the risky fifteen-day flight from England in the Twin Otter and landed by the coastal dump where Simon and Anto had looked after their ice runway throughout the winter and, with great effort, had dug out the 500 fuel drums that Giles would soon be needing. Anto was left to man the dump, but Simon joined the crew as they flew on inland to our near-buried camp at Ryvingen.

Giles brought early Christmas presents for Bothie from his many admirers back home, including the BBC 'Blue Peter' fans, and personal good wishes from Prince Charles. He took his pillowcase of presents to his main bed and there, like an over-excited child, ripped at the paper-clad toys and other tantalising objects. This didn't get him very far, so he became more methodical. Gripping a parcel in his front paws he bit away the Sellotape then, using mouth, teeth and paws, he would unravel the paper and extract the squeaky carrot, pork chop, cat or whatever was inside. There were dog chews and balls of every description and Bothie, quite overcome with excitement, would leap up at each successive discovery and parade a circuit or two around the hut with the item in his teeth before settling down to the next parcel. There were cards galore which I strung up all around his various beds and which he would sniff at with obvious approval, I liked to think, at the memory of this or that person.

My mother, whose name for Bothie from an early age was The Delinquent, had sent him an enormous ball. Remembering what happened to his football in the early months of the winter, I didn't rate its chances highly. But as the sun grew higher in the sky the weather improved and we had many days of hot sun and no wind. On such days Bothie would take the giant ball, nose it up the sliding steps from the radio hut and entertain himself, dribbling it like a professional footballer, trying to climb on top of it, rolling off and chasing it, until, several hours later, he would return to the radio hut, tinkling with clinging iceballs, and retire exhausted to his bed to lick, bite and shake himself free of the ice.

Giles and Gerry flew back to the coast and a front of bad weather held them down there for many days. This was worrying since they had much work ahead to move fuel drums to Ryvingen ready to resupply the ice group. Simon remained with us and wrote in his diary: "Ginnie and Bothie and me running the smallest base in Antarctica . . . Peaceful here with just the three of us." He had not seen Bothie for some eight months and agreed with the air-crew that he had become "an independent-minded little sod".

This, from the somewhat dour Simon, I took to be a term of endearment. Certainly the dog had left his puppyhood behind him during the long hard winter. He had grown tough and lean with especially muscular legs and neck. His hair, responding to the temperature, was now thick and mammoth-like, far more so than the coat of any long-haired Jack Russell at home. He owned a particularly fine set of gnashers and revelled in hanging on to one end of a rubber bone whilst someone, holding the other end, tried

72

Trousers at attention.

Come on, it's supper time.

A sudden insight in Ollie's corner.

Charlie's bark is worse than his bite.

Off-duty snooze.

There must be something I can open

Savouring the mid-winter dinner.

Dawn patrol against the devil dog of Ryvingen.

Bothie jumped in but found he couldn't get out.

to shake his grip. You could lift him, Simon discovered, bodily off the ground and whirl the bone round and round with Bothie glued to it, and growling with delight.

Independent minded he might be, but he was still very lovable; as Giles once put it, "worth a guinea a minute".

Returning once from a re-supply flight to the ice group, and passing over the route that they had travelled the previous week, Giles spotted the wind-accentuated tracks of the skidoos crossing a crevasse, some sixty feet wide where the snow bridge hiding the void below had partially collapsed. Ran, Charlie and Ollie had travelled right over this precarious trap-door, quite unaware of its presence. From the air these crevasses were more obvious as the colour of the snow is different and the long lines show clearly against an otherwise pure white surface. Giles' casual description over the radio as he flew back did nothing to reassure me.

When the weather cleared on the coast it was Ryvingen's turn for a blizzard which shifted tons of snow about the camp, filling porches and tunnel entrances. Bothie and I were trapped in the radio hut for twenty-four hours until a break in the storm allowed the hard-pressed Simon to dig us out.

"Communications are almost impossible," I confessed to Simon above the noise of the hiss and crackle of the receiver, as wind-blown snow caused static on hitting the antenna. "I don't think," I added, "I would even hear them if they did call at the moment." Simon had thoughtfully brought some hot soup which was a wonderful morale boost.

Restored, I sat on for another few hours and Bothie, warmed by the soup, elected to stick it out with me. Then, I heard Ran's voice, calling in to give their daily position, meteorological report and general condition. Bothie, head cocked to one side and ears alert, wagged his tail as first Ran's voice, then Charlie's were recognised.

They were due south of us and 600 miles from the Pole. Their skidoos, sledges and kidneys had been thoroughly rattled and shaken for the last seven hours of slow progress over tortuous sastrugi, two foot high rock-hard ice ridges. Springs and bogey wheels were buckling and sledge runners splitting. They had climbed another 1,500 feet and, although in good spirits, they sounded exhausted. They were also having navigation problems. With no existing maps of the whole region, Ran was hoping to rely on his compass. But there was a large and inconsistent magnetic variation in the area, so now he was trying to use the sun and a home-made sundial scratched on his skidoo windscreen.

The next seventeen days were frustrating. The ice group were caught in a blizzard, no doubt the one that had caused havoc with us. Ten thousand feet above sea level and 600 miles from the Pole, they sat in their small pyramid tent playing cards, sleeping and trying to laugh when I made feeble jokes over the radio in an attempt to take their minds off the weather. Using a small solar panel they could receive radio messages without using too much battery power, but to transmit would have run their batteries down quickly. So I sent them messages from home, and world news stories from the BBC World Service. Nothing seemed to make their voices cheer up. Then I remembered a trick we had taught Bothie during the winter. We would sing out of tune or howl like a wolf and he would soon try to protect his ears by howling in reply. Once he was in full cry, I pressed the transmit button. Within no time there was raucous laughter from the tent. For the next two days Bothie was kept fully employed.

The weeks went by; we were all getting tired. But not

Bothie who remembered that Gerry was a keen cricketer. This meant that balls proffered to Gerry would be sure to fly at great speed and long distances down hard packed snow slopes. Gerry would disparagingly compare "the young squirt" who couldn't even claim any pedigree with his own aristocratic Old English sheepdog. I tried to tell him comparisons were odious, but he would just laugh and lifting his mukluk-covered boot which had Bothie caught up on its toe, he would project the poor little tyke through the air. But Bothie was always able to end his flying lesson with a superb parachute roll, so never came to any harm and always came back for more.

Early in December it seemed that the pin on the radio hut wall-map marking the daily position of the ice group was but an inch from 90° South. Hesitantly, I began to pack away equipment that I would not see again until the Arctic sector of the journey, if ever we got that far. Boxes from all over the camp mounted up by the airstrip for Giles to ferry down to the coastal dump where Anto would take charge of them and go with them back to England. Our furry mascot was thrilled by these activities and quickly sensed something was up as Simon and Gerry rushed back and forth towing loaded sledges.

In the early hours of 15th December Ran called. They had reached the geographical South Pole. They were at 90° South. They'd made it and they knew it was the right place as there was an American base there and they had the best ice cream in the world. Hardly waiting to reply to Ran, I rushed out to shout the news to Simon and Gerry. Simon was on his way back up the hill with Bothie clinging limpet-like to an empty sledge. Thrilled at the news Simon accelerated suddenly and his passenger, caught unaware, catapulted through the air, bounced and rolled into a snowdrift.

Only 300 yards from the Pole the Americans man an all
year research station with a dozen or so scientists who live
in centrally heated huts inside a metal geodesic dome. The
ice group would not be leaving the vicinity of the dome
until we had established a radio base there. Time was now
of the essence. Charlie, Ollie and Ran had more than 1,200
miles to go to the far side of the frozen continent and only
two months left of summer to do it in. Our main concern
was that we might not make it in time and the ship would
not be able to wait for us, but have to leave for another
winter. Ran knew only too well the dangers of lingering
and we all remembered the fate of Captain Scott and his
men who had died so tragically seventy years before on
their way out from the Pole only thirteen short miles from
their depot.

So Simon and I raced to finish packing up and closing
down Ryvingen. Anto came up from the coastal depot to
help and, knowing the ice group were safe at the Pole, we
closed down the radio hut. I drew a map of the camp and
put it with some chocolate bars into a biscuit tin and asked
Simon, our mountaineer, to wedge it securely inside the
framework of the eighty-foot radio mast. If any wandering
visitor were to stumble on our camp it would be good to
think they would be able to make use of it, and find the
entrances to the huts and tunnels! While a brief note about
the composition of our team would reassure them that we
had not all been living on dog food.

Giles and Gerry returned from the coastal dump for the
last time, having left Anto with the last load of cargo to
await the arrival of a South African ship. We loaded the
aircraft with vital equipment. To Giles's disgust this included Bothie. The flight was exceptionally long for a Twin
Otter to attempt, and every single item was weighed,
many 'vital' items having to be discarded if we were going

to have any chance of taking off, let alone reaching the Pole safely. Bothie weighed in at twenty-four pounds (four pounds more than when he left the ship eleven months earlier).

"Oh well," joked Giles, "he'll make good emergency rations I suppose."

Bothie and I were hustled onto the plane, and clutching him protectively I settled him down, wrapped in a parachute, wedged between the fuel tanks and the pilot's seat. Bothie was keen to get the good view he'd had before, but that privileged seat was now taken up by Gerry, so he had to be restrained from trying to climb onto Giles's knee as our pilot gritted his teeth and started the long, bumpy race down the runway to get enough speed for take-off. As we lurched off the rugged strip and clawed our way into the air I took a last look at the little camp that had been our home for so long with a mixture of emotions.

Despite many years of experience flying for the British Antarctic Survey, I wondered whether Giles and Gerry had ever had such an exhausting season as this had been. Giles had made some remarkable flights, including a thousand-mile rescue mission of some South African scientists from a crevasse field and this last take-off could not have been much fun for him. But whenever I find myself in a jumbo jet these days I remember that long flight, and others later, and long for the security of that little aircraft and the confidence we all had in the aircrew to maintain it and fly it.

After the seven-hour flight over featureless plateau cramped in the squat position with Bothie crawling over me and Simon in a similar position opposite, it was a relief to thud down at the South Pole strip. Sick and dizzy, Bothie was handed down to a heavily parka'd American.

"Jeez man," he spat from behind frosted goggles. "They

said nothing about animals." He scrutinised Bothie as he held him head high in the freezing wind. "Is this a dawg?"

Bothie, never able to control his bladder when excited, nearly gave a suitable answer, when he caught the smell of his three long lost friends who approached clad in wolfskin jackets.

"Wooza!" shouted Ollie above the wind. Recognising his nickname, Bothie was off. Caught up in armfuls of wolf fur, he smothered the three men in wet kisses.

Together again, we set up three pyramid tents a hundred yards outside the polar dome and the ex-Marine who was station commander invited us all in for a meal. On noticing a dog running around in the snow he did a double take and, turning to me with a stern expression said, "I'm sorry, but we have strict regulations about animals on this station. We were once donated two huskies by the New Zealand station who thought it would be nice for us to have pets, but we had to send them straight back."

To my everlasting shame I left Bothie in one of our tents and accepted an invitation to have a meal inside the American dome, after being promised a special packet of bones from the kitchen. The gastronomic fantasies we had indulged in during those long winter months were nothing compared with the reality of the polar canteen. Steaks, *fresh* vegetables, fruit, eggs and *milk* – to say nothing of the pump action machine that produced the ice cream that Ran had spoken of.

I cannot pretend that the smell and sight of it all was ruined by the thought of Bothie outside in our tent, and I was tucking into a juicy steak and delicious fresh salad when the canteen cook came over with something hot in silver foil. Gerry took the parcel and, donning his parka, left the warm canteen. An hour later I felt better and went out to the tent. Bloated, and lying on his back, sporting a belly that was visibly stretched to the point of bursting, was Bothie, his head resting lovingly on the boot of the noble Gerry who looked up at me then, pointedly, at his watch. Obviously disgusted with me for neglecting Bothie, he left the tent to go to work on the Twin Otter. Bothie, to show *his* thoughts on the matter, shook himself and, head held high, removed himself from the scene of his debauchery and followed Gerry's tracks through the snow. Thoroughly chastised I gathered up the debris, which alone would have filled Bothie's normal bowl twice over, and returned to the canteen, past the aircraft where Gerry and Bothie were working together on the cargo door.

RAN: Since the Pole camp was short of menial workers, the boss made an agreement with us. If we washed the dishes and kept the canteen clean we could eat with the Americans: a fair deal all round. During the three days it took Ginnie to establish the radio base and Gerry to service the Twin Otter Bothie made hay. One of a small construction gang working on a new camp beside the dome smuggled him into the gangers' dormitory. There he was cosseted, balls were thrown and food fresh from the kitchen was brought out in secret homage. Word of Bothie's location had spread as most of the polar inmates had not seen an animal in months. Whilst everyone inside the dome was a stickler for keeping the rules, the gangers in their own quarters were a rule unto themselves.

Four of us were asked to a gangers' party. On arrival we found Bothie seated in the only armchair, surrounded by admirers feeding him their T-bone steak leftovers. The supply of beer and barbecued sausages was limitless and three guitars were strumming lazy western ditties. Once Bothie associated the gangers with T-bones nothing would keep him away. I did try to cage him inside one of our tents and taped up both skirts. But he simply slipped through one skirt, ripped away the other and escaped, leaving the tent doorless for the second half of the polar crossing.

Each morning Ginnie took him for a walk around the flagpoles of those nations represented in the Antarctic Treaty. Since the flags were planted precisely at the geographic Pole's location, Bothie daily walked round the earth in ten minutes. Gerry the cricketer had his bat and ball with him. Ski-sticks made makeshift stumps and at −33°C, three days before Christmas, our team turned out for a game on a flat space between the Pole and the dome. Bothie favoured the fielding position of silly-mid-on where he was most likely to trap the ball or, as Charlie put it, "get his face smashed in". I never have liked cricket and was thankful when the game was declared a draw with both sides nursing blue noses and fingers. Bothie absconded with the ball which was never seen again. The American scientists were altogether bemused by the whole event and seemed relieved when it was over too. Perhaps they suspected some colonialist ceremony prior to an attempt at raising our Union Jack at 90° South.

Two days before Christmas Ginnie and Gerry completed their work, so there was no further reason for the ice group to delay other than the wonderful festive preparations going on around the base, especially in the kitchen. But my fear of what lay ahead, especially the 9,000-foot glacier we must soon descend, got the better of my craving for turkey and brandy butter. So Charlie, Ollie and I left the Pole and headed due north. This was not difficult since due north lay directly ahead no matter where you looked.

This time Bothie was quite unconcerned to see us depart. He had smelled mouth-watering dreamlike whiffs emanat-

A word in Charlie's ear.

Bagged up to hunt for the abandoned South African camp.

Summer morning on the skidoo tracks.

Ollie and Bothie check a crevasse ladder for safety.

Superdog rearranging the Antarctic icecap.

The ice group have gone south, Bothie's in charge.

ing from the construction camp and knew another beautiful experience was just around the corner. After eight
months of frozen addled eggs, he surely deserved a
Christmas feast.

GINNIE: Bothie was the life and soul of some fairly wild
Christmas festivities, including a sledge circuit of the
station by assorted scientists, gangers and Bothie sitting
on top of it, and a tobogganing competition from the top
of the 200-foot dome. Bothie was disqualified because he
tumbled off his toboggan near the top of the dome and
free rolled most of the way down the snowdrift.

On the evening of Christmas day I was able to report,
"They're at the top of Scott Glacier."

This meant the ice group had successfully traversed the
entire Antarctic icecap and reached its far rim. But this rim
was 9,000 feet above the Ross Ice Shelf and the glacier
which poured down in successive icefalls was riven by the
worst crevasses they were to face anywhere.

So while the polar dome reverberated to carols, bawdy
songs and great revelry, Bothie joined me from the partying
and we began our long vigil by the radio as Ran, Ollie and
Charlie inched their way down serrated icefalls and over
nightmare caverns. Giles, although at the party, was aware
of the possibilities and was remaining sober on some
odd-coloured drink he had become particularly partial to.

RAN: Oliver nearly managed to kill himself twice but each
time luck rather than good management on our part came
to his rescue. We learnt that it is possible to sweat at −30°C
without doing anything but sit on a skidoo and drive over
rotten snowbridges. Never were the three of us more
thankful than when on the morning of the third day's
descent we saw the distant horizon of the Ross Ice Shelf
below and some thirty broken miles ahead. That same
evening after ten desperate hours, the last mountain range

fell away to our flank and we emerged onto the relative safety of the ice shelf.

GINNIE: For forty-eight hours I heard nothing. Americans popped in and out at all times of day and night to enquire if there was any news. They had become caught up in the drama and bets were being made all over the camp as to whether our ice group would make it and how soon. The general consensus was that *if* they survived it would take from ten to fourteen days.

After receiving Ran's call I crept along the corridor to the base commander's office where he was working late and told him the news they were safely at the bottom and on the Ross Ice Shelf. A great deal of money was lost at the Pole, but it didn't get in the way of genuine relief and enthusiasm which was typical of our warm-hearted hosts. On Giles's next flight to resupply the ice group were all kinds of goodies and messages of congratulation, as they rested for a day at the foot of Scott Glacier and enjoyed a well deserved New Year celebration.

After a memorable Christmas we said goodbye to our Pole friends. The base commander's eye twinkled as he shook Bothie's paw. "Come again some day," he whispered.

We flew over many awesome unnamed mountains and glaciers until the Twin Otter's shadow danced on the slopes of Mount Erebus, the only active volcano in Antarctica. Below the 13,000-foot smoking cone, Giles landed within sight of Scott Base where New Zealand scientists work. They had kindly agreed to house four people and one terrier.

Bothie was glad to be aground. His ears had been painful during the descent to sea level and he had cowered with his paws over them like the 'Hear-no-evil' monkey. Scott Base, a huddle of green wooden huts, nestled on gravel benchland where Ross Island joins the sea-ice. Some years, even in summer, the ice here does not break up, but we saw many open fissures and fat Weddel seals lying about new waterholes. They were not the only animal life around. As we drove towards the camp in an old jeep the howls of huskies sounded wolf-like in the distance. Bothie sniffed the air nervously.

Somebody had kindly built Bothie a kennel of varnished pine, with the Scott Base symbol of a rampant penguin painted on one side and, on the other, still drying in the sun, Bothie's name and the date he arrived after crossing Antarctica. As we walked through the camp to find Bothie's new hutch, the tail of this intrepid hound suddenly disappeared between his legs and his diminutive body hit the deck. I grabbed the wilting hero and stood stock still as two enormous evil smelling hounds bounded up. Simultaneously the wide hairy forepaws of the two werewolves were upon me. Terror struck Bothie, and I stood like Lot's wife on Sodom hill. Someone laughed, inappropriately I felt, but then a gruff, bearded character grabbed one of the devil dogs.

"They're only puppies," he said, still grinning as he pulled the second dog away. The two creatures mercifully lolloped off after him.

"That's Doggo," smiled our guide. "He looks after our husky teams. The puppies are OK."

"You could have fooled me," I croaked, still shaking from the experience. I watched closely to ascertain where the 'puppies' went and was reassured to see them put into a cage.

Bothie's new kennel was outside the hut assigned to me, the size of a garden shed but equipped with a comfortable bed and heater bar. When taken by the urge to wander, Bothie simply towed the kennel to which he was tied, behind him over the snow. I often found the vagrant down by the rubbish dump. One memorable evening four recently discarded chicken carcasses lay a few yards in front of his straining jowls, but his kennel was jammed between two bits of rubbish and all he could do was observe in frustration the gluttony of numerous skuas.

Scott Base is within easy walking distance of many famous landmarks left by the early expeditions – Observation Hill, Castle Rock and the old wooden hut that served as a refuge to Scott's men for so long. In places storms had blown the winter snow away exposing bare rock. Bothie loved these spots, rolling on his back from side to side and barking with joy. Perhaps he had begun to fear that all the world had disappeared under a coverlet of snow.

One area he did not like to visit was the ice foot below the base. The huskies were kept there chained to stakes along the shoreline. Each was carefully tethered out of fang-range of the next. The first, and last, time we went for a walk past them two dozen or so dogs, baring outsize molars, flung themselves bodily against their chains. They growled and barked with maximum ferocity and leapt from side to side, their forepaws clawing the air. Bothie, never a dog who could be cajoled into walking to heel, became a model of good behaviour by walking so close to my booted shins that he tripped me up.

Further along the ice foot, rifle shots rang out over the sea-ice. Doggo was shooting his annual allotment of sixty seals for husky meat during the coming winter. A rank and unpleasant smell of salty slaughter came over the fields of rolling pressure ice and two intrepid Transglobers decided unanimously to go no further.

To restore the terrier's pride we entered him for the annual Scott Hut Race which is open to all inhabitants of

Scott Base and the neighbouring American McMurdo Station which shares occupancy of Ross Island. There were over a hundred hopeful entrants, Bothie being the only British competitor, plus of course his minder (Simon) to whom he was attached by a cord. Sadly Simon had hurt his knee and held Bothie back which, as we explained later to the ship's crew, was the only reason they did not come away with the prize.

On returning to the camp on the back of an open truck he stood quivering with vengeful passion, every muscle in his tiny body rippling with tension, as he yapped furious revenge at the demented huskies straining dangerously at their chains. The laughter and cheers of his Kiwi travelling companions increased the frenetic yapping of the terrier, which in turn increased the husky howls of anguish.

That evening the ice group wearily ended a 700-mile traverse of the Ross Ice Shelf. They had crossed Antarctica on open vehicles in sixty-seven days.

RAN: At first we had detoured wide about a horrendous region known as the Steershead Crevasses, then for many days, we lost sight of the coastal mountains altogether and saw nothing but flat horizons of whiteness. Above Mount Erebus a volcanic cloud steamed with the wind against a sky of magical blue and for a whole day we inched onwards, steering by the cloud alone. Then the great volcano itself came into view, at a hundred miles a mere white pyramid, flanked soon by the hump of Minna Bluff and the twin humps of White Island and Black Island – all sights which in living memory had meant food, warmth and survival to returning explorers of Scott's company.

GINNIE: As the ice group grew into three black dots the men and women of Scott Base left what they were doing and one by one came out in their parkas to the ledge of gravel between the huts and the mainland. A piper struck up a tune that keened out over the ice and on cue Bothie raised his eyes to heaven and bayed. Doggo hitched a slender Nansen sled to his huskies and mushed them to a ragged canter over the sea-ice.

"They're here," I explained to a mystified Bothie who was unaware what all the fuss was about and thinking only of his grumbling stomach after the stresses of trying to pull Simon round the hilly race course.

The ice group followed Doggo's yapping team over loosening floes and past curious seals to the ice foot where there was much back slapping, camera clicking and mutual fostering of Anglo-Kiwi relations. The longest crossing of Antarctica and the only one on open vehicles, was over. The expedition's first obstacle was behind us.

One fine blustery morning out at Hut Point where, month after month, Scott's weary men had stared out to sea in vain, we waited with Bothie, straining our eyes over the ice in McMurdo Sound.

What a wonderful sight – the two masts and stubby funnel of the *Benjamin Bowring*, great blocks of loose ice crumbling under her bow as she moved towards us, now and again a glint of water exploding from the black backs of killer whales. From the ship's loudspeaker as she neared us came the strains of 'Land of Hope and Glory'. She manoeuvred into the ice-choked bay directly below Scott's hut and made fast to a man-made ice pontoon.

Bothie was first up the gangplank to the cheers of all on board. A great deal of patting, hugging and, on his part, licking followed as all his old friends greeted him.

The ship zinged with the most fascinating smells. The past year she had plied the Samoan coral isles as a trader and the scent of Fakfau coconut, Funafuti chicken, Atatu yam and Nuknonu piglet lingered above and below deck. All day long, rubber balls forgotten, Bothie patrolled the ship, tail up and nostrils aquiver. After the long months of monochrome, there was once again a wealth of colour and excitement to his life.

6

Dog Days on the Yukon

GINNIE: Along the seaward edge of Ross Island, our ship hove to by Cape Evans, site of Scott's last winter home and faithfully preserved during recent years by visiting New Zealanders. A brooding atmosphere emanated from the volcanic mounds about the hut and the ceaseless stirring in the penguin rookery above. Dark on the lobby floor sprawled a seventy-year-old supply of seal blubber; penguin eggs, gathered for food, now lay forgotten in a box, their contents shrivelled and evaporated. The hut inmates who once had laughed and dared, striven and suffered in their epic venture, all within living memory, were now dead like their dogs and horses, whose harnesses and foot pads hung from the rafters. We left the wild cape quietened after our brief dip into the congealed paintpot of history.

Back on board, Bothie brought us back to reality as he yapped at the penguins waddling along the ice beside the ship, their usually sleek coats now tattered and moth-eaten in moult.

The Roaring Forties ensured that a number of passengers were abed and suffering, but not Transglobe's terrier. From dawn to dusk he trotted the gangways, patrolled the bridge, skidded about the heaving saloon floor and generally asserted his presence.

Did you hear them calling?

They're very faint.

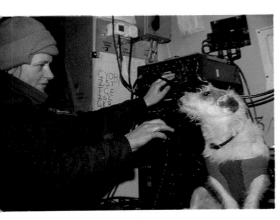

Tune it up, will you.

She's taking her time.

Ah, it's for me.

Shall I howl them a song?

I supervise the network. She just changes the frequencies.

South Pole, 15th December 1980: the first terrier at the bottom of the world.

Bothie's off limits tent at the South Pole.

Cricket at the South Pole with Bothie at silly-mid-on.

First up the gangplank at Scott Base after a year in Antarctica

Several days later a bleak mist-curled island rose above the ship. Anton held the excited terrier under one arm, his other on the helm and, for the first time in over a year, the dog saw what he had smelled – vegetation, lashings of it. Not just beds of wave-washed kelp, playground of elephant seals, but cliffs crowned with *grass* and stubby trees. Bothie went wild, galloping about the bridge carpet in tight circles, knowing that his nose and eyes couldn't both be deceiving him. Great was his despondency thirty minutes later, when two dozen Transglobers took the lifeboat ashore, leaving him on board with only the skipper and a couple of the least venturesome for company.

Campbell Island has no permanent human inhabitants. It is a nature reserve where visiting ships are not normally allowed to disembark, but someone had made an exception for us and we were able to savour this perfect, unspoilt sub-Antarctic island. A handful of annually rotated Kiwi scientists, mostly zoologists, run a cosy base at the head of a sea fjord and they were pleased to see strangers. Not that we had much news for them of the world at large. They showed us hidden bays where stinking sea elephants wallowed and pretty sea lions played, and grassy clifftops alive with the brittle 'quaark' of the nesting Royal albatross, a huge but gentle bird. Pure white and very noble, they allowed the zoologist with us to lift them off their nests to reveal eggs and newly hatched chicks.

A handful of grass was smuggled back on board for the frustrated Bothie and was scattered to the four winds as the horny hound went berserk. That same evening our ship took us away from the shelter of the island and two more days of non-stop buffeting saw us abeam the New Zealand coast. It was raining a warm drizzle and the local dockers' union was on strike, so those of us from Britain felt very much at home, and Bothie rolled in the puddles on deck.

The little dog waxed delirious as land-based smells washed over the ship, but once again he watched in hurt silence as everybody went ashore without him. We tried hard to budge bureaucracy but the rules were rigid. *No dogs.* Maybe this one had been on a disease-free continent for a year but you never knew. Better safe than sorry.

Wherever we stopped during the expedition we set up an exhibition in the largest available harbourside hall. In Auckland the Prime Minister, Robert Muldoon, officially opened the exhibit and I tried pleading with him for Bothie's release, but to no avail. He was already getting flak from many quarters for allowing the South African Springboks in to play rugby and he couldn't see his way to taking more by allowing one English mongrel ashore. Twenty-four thousand visitors crammed through our show during the next five days and from a balcony that overlooked the ship, they waved at the crew members on deck watch, which of course included Bothie the guard dog. Many of them had heard about his adventures in the Antarctic and called out to see the dog phenomenon. So every hour the bosun toured the deck alongside a specially spruced-up terrier, ending up on the fo'c's'le where they both waved at the crowd in a regal fashion as cameras clicked.

Some visitors were allowed on board as many had provided free paint, eggs, beer etc. Wherever we went it was Anton's job to replenish all ship's stores at no cost. Bothie made certain that he personally greeted and vetted all strangers at the top of the gangplank with a ball or squeaky toy in his mouth, and stayed with them until they parted with some token of their goodwill. Those that had nothing to give were advised by crew members to proffer some scrap from the kitchen or throw his ball down the gangways because, as the bosun used to say, "The little sod is getting mean, what with being stuck on board like a prisoner while the rest of the crew live it up ashore." One little girl, Daisy, came back day after day to play with Bothie and to this day any pretty blonde, about five years old, is a prime target for Bothie's attention.

In an attempt to alleviate his shipbound frustration, I brought a bagful of offerings on board, small branches of pine tree to play with, a box of earth to spray all over the bosun's newly painted deck and, most appreciated of all, a sack of straw. I found a huge cardboard box to pour it into and he burrowed his way deep into its scratchy, sweet-smelling contents, rolling, biting, chewing and finally subsiding ecstatically, deep into his new aromatic bunk to sleep and no doubt dream of the real world. A choir of comely grass-skirted Maori girls sang us away from their bountiful land with a haunting tune that wished us love and luck, 'Arohatinani'.

Our next port of call was Sydney. We had five Kiwi crew members who all agreed the Aussies would be a push-over compared with the Auckland bureaucrats.

"No bother. They'll let the woofter off. Just get the skipper to square the port veterinary fella with some pommie beer. That'll give him the chance to tell you all how much better the Aussie stuff is."

The Kiwis were wrong about their neighbours who turned out to be equally rigid. Bothie had to sweat out a further confinement aboard in Sydney harbour, a stone's throw from the cool white curves of the city's opera house. But here he could at least maintain a constant vigil on the boat deck, venting his frustrations on any seagulls that dared to enter within two feet of his airspace. There were sailing boats galore, and motor boats to watch and exchange greetings with, which kept him fully entertained between his public appearances. Australia has a large Jack

Russell Club whose supporters had sent messages to him in the Antarctic, so he made a special effort to look his best for them, especially when one of their number arrived on the quayside with two very attractive Jack Russell bitches.

Our enjoyment of Sydney was tinged with the sadness of knowing that Ollie, with whom we had all shared so much, was going to have to leave the expedition at this point for personal reasons and return to England. But before he went there were to be two expedition weddings and a visit from our Patron.

Prince Charles, who had just announced his engagement to Lady Diana Spencer, came on board to ask how things were going and say hello to all the team. After a quarter of an hour's chatting to the crew, His Royal Highness had still not spoken to Bothie who was in an evil mood after the heavy session of enforced shampooing in the galley sink. The team were lined up in order of naval seniority, which means the bosun comes before the cabin boy, if you have one. So Bothie was at the far end of the line. Everyone had agreed this was perfectly fair since the dog had no known naval skills. But Bothie decided the whole deal was outrageous and cut right across a remark the Prince was addressing to the skipper with a furious barrage of yap-yaps.

Our Patron spent the next two minutes on his haunches in private conversation with the demonstrative tyke, the latter's front paws up on his pin-striped knee. Mollified, he behaved for the rest of the royal visit and when the crew gave Prince Charles a small wedding gift, he joined in the three cheers with hearty barks of approval.

Missing out on two wedding ceremonies was a bitter pill for Bothie. I'm sure he felt he should have been best man, or at least a page, as Charlie was to marry a girl to whom he had popped the question shortly before the expedition began, and Anton was to marry our ship's cook, Jill, whom he had wooed during the charter period in the Pacific.

Bothie determined to gatecrash the ceremonies. He sat down and methodically chewed through the rope that secured him to the boat deck where he kept guard at the top of the gangway. Being cunning not to attract the attention of the watchkeeper left on board, he slipped quietly down the gangplank to the quayside. But on reaching the road he must have lost his calm with the forgotten sound of cars rushing back and forth. He was spotted and gathered up by a concerned cyclist who handed him over to the police.

Furious, hot and thirsty, he was returned to the ship and resecured to his chewed rope. Within two hours, in the midst of Anton and Jill's reception on the boat deck, a Port Authority Pest Control Officer came on board, carrying a chain that could have restrained a bull mastiff. With this he lashed Bothie to the rail and gave firm instructions that he must not be released until the ship sailed, departing to the boos and hisses of the wedding party and the furious growl-barks of Bothie. Once he had gone Bothie recovered from the imputations of pest control by gorging himself on shrimps, cheese chunks and sausages, washed down with sips of champagne from a saucer.

The day before we left Sydney I noticed Ollie sitting in the saloon with Bothie standing on his lap, front paws on his shoulders. The two were nose to nose. Ollie was talking to the dog, saying goodbye. The next morning he left the ship for good and Bothie lost one of his closest friends.

I too had to return to England to hand over the results of the VLF magnetospheric research we had done in Ryvingen. I would rejoin the ship in Los Angeles, but before going I instructed Ran in the subtleties of feeding and exercising Bothie, and left a big bag of sweets, toys, chews and bones in our cabin – to console one another with, I thought, during the next few weeks, misguidedly assuming they would miss me as much as I knew I would miss them. I also left with Anton an Easter egg for Ran and a large rubber squeaky chicken for Bothie as Easter was only a few days away.

RAN: We sailed north-east of the Great Barrier Reef out towards Suva and rolled day after day through torpid heat and a flat brassy sea. Flying fish expired on deck where melted tar ran along the plank seams. Dolphins raced and plunged, moving far faster than the ship. Even by night the heat was oppressive. Some of us slept on mats on deck.

To the crew the heat was nothing after their long months working the coral isles of Samoa. Whilst we had shivered on the icecap, they had suffered prickly heat rash in the South Pacific, earning enough charter money to keep the ship solvent. But Bothie was now a polar dog and found the heat exhausting, for nowhere on board was there an air-conditioned corner. In my equipment hold it was as airy as anywhere and I often carried him down with me when working on the gear for the Yukon and the Arctic. Normally I did not trust him down below, for there were pellets of rat poison in every corner, usually being ignored by the company of ship's mice. But now Bothie simply collapsed on the concrete ballast floor and lay there hour after hour panting hard with his long pink tongue lolling loose.

Sometimes the skipper allowed us all a delicious dip in the sea by heaving to in a gentle swell. Brown bodies plunged off the deck rails and bobbed about, eyes wary for shark fins. Bothie inched his way down the gangplank which had been lowered for the swimmers to climb aboard. I didn't think for a minute he would dare to jump in as the ship rolled and lurched in a heavy swell, but in case he fell in, a rope was attached to his harness. Feeling the security of this he went further down the slippery gangplank until, as the ship rolled, his little legs were immersed in the cool green water. The sheer ecstasy drove him to irresponsible action. The ship rolled again and he took off, flinging his tubby frame into a spectacular belly flop before sinking below the surface. Someone grabbed the rope, but before they could bring him back on board he was swimming wildly, thrashing at the surface with his little paws and thoroughly enjoying it. Cheers from the crew encouraged him and he turned away from the ship, upper lip curled back in a grin showing teeth gritted with determination. After some minutes, although he was still swimming hard, his head began to disappear and he sank below the surface, his nose thrown up to the sky. He was quickly yanked out on the rope. Simon, who was beside him at the time, said he just got waterlogged with his massive coat. But his esteem went up several notches as a result of this escapade and his jocular gait carried him proudly back up the gang-plank, water streaming from his fur, to the saloon where he shook himself all over the floor.

He had never crossed the Equator on a ship before so, as we inched over that invisible half-way mark, and the strange maritime rituals and drunken ceremonies got under way, Bothie was included amongst the victims. Sticky green gunk was applied by King Neptune's court jester, whilst the Queen, a deckie with supercargo of two football bladders under his shirt, thrust her cardboard trident menacingly at the waiting line of victims. These were few in number since most of the crew had crossed the line many times before. Bothie enjoyed the event because it was cool and followed by a long shower, as I tried to get the ceremonial gunk out of his thick post-polar coat.

A month later we reached the United States coastline and cleft through a sea alive with billions of tiny jellyfish. In the heart of Los Angeles dockland Mayor Bradley welcomed us with a gift of the city's key, all ten brass inches of it, and we set up our exhibition in a passenger terminal which once had welcomed many millions of European refugees to the free land of their dreams, and was to prove the free land of Bothie's dreams as well.

"This is truly a free country," Ginnie said when she met us as the ship pulled alongside. "Guess what?"

"You've taken out US citizenship," I suggested.

"No, you nana. He's allowed out! He's free!"

"Who?"

Ginnie threw a shoe at me. "Bothie, of course. They say he can go wherever he wants so long as he obeys the laws of the land." And she rushed off to tell the happy news to Bothie himself. If she'd expected him to dance a jig of delight she was not disappointed.

As soon as Bothie reached the bottom of the gangplank, stubby tail wagging so fast it was a mere white blur, he raced off in no special direction, nose glued to the quayside, dilated nostrils drinking in every delicious-disgusting smell. He came up short beside a lamp-post, a real live post with a lamp on it (or at least a smashed fluorescent bulb, but who's arguing), and with an entirely reflex action, his starboard leg shot into the air to the horizontal and there he waited, lips drawn back over fangs in a fixed grin.

Several of the crew up on deck broke into a cheer, much to Ginnie's embarrassment. However even this verbal encouragement did not help anything materialise. Determined to bless this, his first lamp-post in two years, the terrier remained frozen in his three-legged stance and ignored Ginnie's calls. Thinking he had cramp, she eventually clipped a lead to his collar and dragged him away with

Scott's Hut at Cape Evans.

Fun and games on 'the lawn' in mid-Pacific.

South Pacific bathing party.

one leg still in the air, like a plump hopeful auditioning for the corps de ballet.

On the far side of the passenger terminal they found a patch of grass. It was brown and dusty and littered with fag-ends but it *was* grass. Unclipped, Bothie rolled ecstatically over and over in the mucky patch. Then, on his back, he wiggled his bottom about until he was thoroughly dirty. Next came the rutting deer stuff, the violent scratching up of dust with the back legs, accompanied by a fierce bout of deep Alsatian-type growling. By now Ginnie could see nothing but a whirling dustcloud.

An hour later a grimy, exhausted, but exhilarated little mongrel was hauled back on board. Too excited to eat, he lay outstretched on the saloon floor – straining at his lead, his tail, eyes, lips and nostrils twitching with anticipation as he waited for someone to release him.

Ginnie and Bothie had to go for some injections in Los Angeles because after the ship reached Vancouver they would be land based again, driving north to a rendezvous on the Yukon. Bothie's shots included a rabies jab which was painful. However he took it like a dog and was rewarded with the promise of a night in a luxury suite on board the *Queen Mary*. All the team were being given free accommodation for a week on the impressive old P. & O. liner, but dogs were forbidden.

"Do you realise," Ginnie pointed out, "the poor dog will not have another comfortable night for the next eighteen months?"

"So what?" I said. "He's a dog. It's not as if he knows this is the *Queen Mary*."

"Of course he does and he *is* coming on board," Ginnie retorted. Trying to cringe myself into the old marine paintwork, I followed Ginnie, plus dog on a tight lead, up numerous red carpeted stairways and beneath a barrage of 'NO DOGS' signs until, sweating profusely, I realised we had made it past the busy reception desk. Ginnie ran down the long carpeted passage to our cabin as I tried to fill the whole width of the corridor with myself and my coat to hide the white backside scurrying along beside her.

Bothie's 'night of comfort' needless to say became five nights and somehow nobody ever challenged Ginnie as she brazenly led the dirty pooch up and down the plush corridors of the old Queen.

GINNIE: He was not dirty! He had a bath every night to cool him down and spruce him up for the exhibition, and never once misbehaved. He talked to the life-like sailor robot and barked happily at the seagulls from our cabin porthole. He was in seventh heaven and slept, not where he was put, but on the spare bed in our dressing room.

North of Los Angeles our old ship slipped into cooler climes. Bothie spent long hours on the plastic green lawn which Dave Hicks the steward had spread out on the boat deck. He lay there like a retired gaffer staring out to sea, his head resting on his forepaws, his back legs stretched out behind. Many a time I saw the more lonely members of the crew going to sit on the bench beside him, also scanning the empty horizons and no longer feeling alone.

With Vancouver Island to port we crossed the 49th parallel and entered Canadian waters. Bothie was welcomed into British Columbia by a bevy of press photographers whom he ignored. A cat had appeared fleetingly on the quayside. The ensuing chase was one-sided because the terrier's speed and hunting skills were rusty from lack of practice in Antarctica. The cat escaped, but in a fluid manoeuvre a cat would have admired our wily sea dog camouflaged his aborted intentions under the guise of a general quay reconnaissance, thus keeping the honour of the ship's company intact.

Bothie and I were now to take to the open road. We would be driving a support Land Rover up through the Yukon, Alaska and the North West Territory, keeping in radio contact with Ran and Charlie as they boated up the Yukon and negotiated the formidable challenge of the North-West Passage.

In addition to the radio, with a telescopic aerial fixed to the rear of the vehicle, we had to carry resupply items and spares and base camp equipment for the next two months. By the time we had loaded ten full petrol cans, two water cans, spare wheels, ration boxes and two forty-horse power outboard engines, there was already an overload problem. By judicious use of roof rack, trailer and even the passenger seat, I was finally ready, providing Bothie travelled half on my lap and half astride the gear lever.

Simon Grimes was to stay in Vancouver for a while and later find his own way north to join Bothie and me. The rest of the team left on the ship which we wouldn't see again for at least another year. The *Benjamin Bowring* sailed north along the rugged British Columbia coast, through the Aleutian Islands and into the Bering Straits between the USSR and Alaska. Somewhere off the mouth of the Yukon River in mid-June, by which time the spring break-up should have cleared, Ran and Charlie would be dropped overboard with two twelve-foot inflatable rubber boats, outboards and 900 pounds of equipment each. By river and sea they would have the three short months of summer to traverse some 5,000 miles north of the Arctic Circle and, with luck, reach the northern edge of Ellesmere Island before the sea froze for the winter.

British Columbia is bigger than ten Switzerlands, plus Great Britain, yet there are a mere 3,000,000 inhabitants; most of them in one corner of the state. There are very few roads and the vast majority of them are untarmac-ed. The pleasant dearth of humans is more than compensated for by billions of insects which range from monster clegs, known as moose flies, with a bite like a mule-kick, to no-see-ums, hardly visible midges whose bites produce a grade-ten itch. Small wonder that so many inhabitants of the region, whether Indians, white trappers or oilmen, seek to harden their skin through consumption of amazing quantities of alcohol.

The expedition dog and radio operator advanced north via the Alaska Highway, sleeping little and heating up tins of sardines beside the vehicle whilst making the daily radio call to the ship as it advanced up the coast. The further north we went the more the bugs increased. Bothie, growing tired of his position straddled across the gear stick, had pushed a hole for himself atop the boxes and sleeping bag roll behind my head where he had a giddy view of our route. But he enjoyed the cool breeze that blew on his face and soon nestled down to sleep.

After several days I noticed he had become restless and was biting himself and scratching. I had thought he was well protected from the hungry insects, but found his stomach covered in a mass of red pimples, and around his ears and nose too there were signs of irritation. Without as much protective fur, I suffered even more than Bothie. I anointed us both with citronella oil each morning, but the relentless mozzies homed in on it as if for an aperitif. In the end I took refuge in isolated motels. Bothie would swim happily in my bath water which seemed to help his bites and then settle down to nibble his stomach and try to remove the irritating lumps – several times he got carried away and would let out a yelp of pain as he nipped one of his more delicate appendages by mistake.

Much to my embarrassment, Bothie's oversexed nature came to the fore at these motel refuelling stops. Many drivers on the Alaska Highway had plastered their back windows with 'ALASKA OR BUST' or 'WE DROVE THE ALASKA HIGHWAY' stickers, as though it were the uttermost limits of the known world. They also tended to own outsized dogs. Bothie just loves large dogs. Male or female he doesn't mind. He was not in the least impressed by bared fangs, and went straight for a leg, front, back, left or right, it didn't matter, and clung on like a limpet-mine. On one occasion a particularly large and fluffy St Bernard continued to amble about the motel restaurant quite unaware that a small white terrier was clamped to his front left leg.

I studiously ignored these happenings and immersed myself in sunny-side-up and pecan pie. But I did remove the Union Jack sticker from our rear window before we drove off.

In the middle of pine-clad nowheres, punctures forced the now weary travellers to halt and get thoroughly bitten whilst changing tyres. Then the trailer's axle snapped, conveniently close to a remote fishing competition. A kind fisherman drove me to a remote phone-box from where I telephoned one of my brothers who happened to live in a remote log home not far away. Like all Canadians, he owned a pick-up truck and soon arrived to rescue his long-lost sister whom he hadn't seen for twelve years.

The trailer was pronounced irreparable but a U-haul trailer company agreed to rent out a replacement in three days' time. Whilst waiting, Bothie and I stayed with my brother whose dog made friends with mine. Together they hunted in the forest beside the house until a black bear chased them right down out of the wood to the vegetable garden. The goat, who roamed the garden and provided fresh milk for the family, became the next centre of attraction. When tired of the exercise of avoiding the goat's butting horns, Bothie would amble over to a large run where my brother bred rabbits. Breeding's something rabbits are good at and Bothie would sit for hours mesmerised by this moving mass of brown bunny, until one strayed from the mass to a corner to snooze. Then the mighty hunter would go into a crouch, pounce, and reel back to nurse a nose bruised against the wire netting. There was also a cunning cat who teased him by hiding under the verandah, and chickens, cockerels and a duck to be sent squawking, quacking and flapping into the trees.

With the rented trailer in tow, my brother said a cool farewell to Bothie and our journey continued over the Yukon border and finally, to Dawson City, fabled sin city of the gold rush days.

My limited pocket money was depleted because of the motel stops and so I sought employment at the Klondike Lodge, self-styled gateway to the far north, where the Yukon and Klondike rivers converge. The proprietors of this very busy motel-cum-truck repair shop adopted us like long lost friends, and generously agreed that I could use their telephone to receive calls from our London office in return for making beds, washing up and serving coffee in the café. We could also eat in the canteen and use their washing machine which was wonderful as we had grown tired of sardines and baked beans and my sleeping bag was full of dust and Bothie hairs. At night I slept in the rear of the Land Rover in the car park, with Bothie stretched out on the driver's seat.

Using the 100-watt radio and a mast, I made contact with Ran a thousand miles to the west. His news was all of delays. One of the ship's engine tiebolts had sheared in the Bering Sea. Charlie's inflatables had capsized off the Yukon River mouth and a disaster only narrowly averted. Then unusually high winds had turned certain canyons on the river into cauldrons. Every lost day lessened their chances of getting to our Arctic base at Alert before winter clamped down. The spectre of failure loomed large.

I continued to make beds and serve coffee and took Bothie for long walks where he marvelled at chipmunks and other strange new smells. Swimming in the cold rushing waters of the Klondike helped to soothe his itching bites and clear his coat of the cloying red dust. He was greatly amused as trout slid under him in the crystal water, oblivious to the four stubby thrashing legs above.

One evening a clumsy moose blundered out of the trees into the clearing and came eyeball to eyeball with the bathing party. Bothie, no larger in total than the great beast's head, kept his nerve and stood rigid, every muscle flexed. A low throaty growl through bared fangs developed into an hysterical yap. The moose, evidently stunned by the horrendous experience, turned with a snort and returned whence he came. Later that week I realised the risks I'd been taking in my greenhorn way when reports of two canoeists being mauled and killed as they camped beside the Yukon buzzed round the hotel café. After that I threw Bothie's ball into a large rain puddle in the car park instead.

But soon he was lucky to get that much attention. Ran's voice on the radio sounded strained. "We must get a whaler," he said. "These inflatables are too slow." So I was commissioned to conjure up from somewhere a sixteen-foot two-man fibre-glass whaler, for free of course, and have it delivered to Inuvik on the Mackenzie River. This took two weeks and a lot of long distance talking, but eventually it was on its way, and so were we.

We drove all day over mountain ranges, through tiny mining camps, across the Yukon/Alaska border and stopped at one of the few fuel pumps, in solitary splendour beside a shop-cum-post office-cum-bar that was known as Chicken. Bothie settled down to eat some cold hamburgers, a parting gift to him from our good friends at Klondike Lodge, while I had a tyre replaced. A can of Coke, some black coffee, a bowl of water and an irresistible T-shirt inscribed with a chicken hatching out of its egg above the words 'I WAS LAID IN CHICKEN, ALASKA', and we were off again to Fairbanks. Somewhere, hundreds of miles to the north, we would cross the Yukon River by way of the Yukon River Bridge and there we would hope to find Ran and Charlie.

RAN: Charlie and I arrived at the bridge, pulled the inflatables onto the bank and brewed up some tea whilst we waited for Ginnie. We had travelled well over a thousand miles by river in the last few weeks since leaving the ship in the Bering Straits. We must now press on north by the newly opened, but not yet paved, Dempster Highway to the Mackenzie River at Inuvik. A week's delay at this stage could lose us a year.

High above us we heard the Land Rover wheels humming over the planks of the enormous bridge and saw Ginnie waving out of the window. Deflating the inflatables, everyone worked to transfer the cargoes to trailer and roof rack, encouraged by clouds of mosquitoes and the yapping of Bothie, not, as you might think, overjoyed at the family reunion, but demanding help to reach one of the big fish hanging nearby to dry on wooden racks erected by the local Indian fishermen.

We soon learnt that the new road north was impassable with floods, so for four precious days we cooled our heels, exploring the old gold rush camps and even tried our luck at Diamond Tooth Gertie's gambling parlour back in Dawson City. On the fifth day confirmation came through that the flood damage had been repaired and we set off.

Relics of the Klondike gold rush.

Ran-hauling off the Mackenzie River sandbanks.

Bothie meets the scavenging sisters of Tuktoyaktuk.

Evenly matched, if not for long.

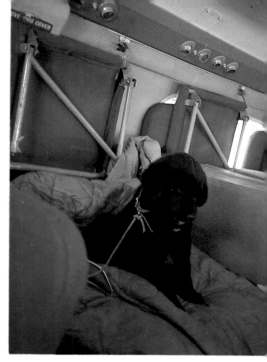

Blackdog received a mixed welcc
at Cambridge Bay.

The start of a long affair.

Beach watch for Ran and Charlie at Tanquary Fjord.

The whaler that made it through the North-West Passage.

A day later we crossed the Mackenzie River ferry and reached the thriving Indian settlement of Inuvik.

Simon and the whaler had arrived by air and we transported the fibre-glass boat to the river with care. It would be our sole means of transport and survival for the next 3,000 miles. A shallow draft barge chugged twice weekly between Inuvik and an Eskimo settlement, Tuktoyaktuk, at the mouth of the Mackenzie River. Simon packed all the equipment from the Land Rover onto the barge and went with it. David Mason would later arrange for his brother to drive the Land Rover back to the ship at Vancouver, an expedition in itself.

Bothie took the whaler in his stride. It had two motors which made an alarming noise but no more so than the lawn mower in London. The wide river was choppy, sometimes quite rough, but what was that to a dog who had braved the worst the Atlantic and Pacific had to offer. He settled down on the narrow canvas awning athwart the bows and allowed his eyes to glaze over in the chilly sunlight. He opened them again three hours later to find the river was over a mile wide, that the best heading to take was being discussed busily by Ginnie and Charlie and that his master was ten yards away, wading up to his knees in the muddy water, and pulling the whaler off a sandbank into which someone had unknowingly steered. Bothie decided to keep awake.

After many more false trails, the motley whaler crew arrived, late in the day, at the river's mouth and Canada's northern coastline – all wet to the waist, except Bothie who was wet all over, after taking it in turns to pull the whaler off successive sandbanks. From this point the boat would have to head east along the notorious route between Arctic islands that make up the North-West Passage.

Many have died in this passage over the centuries.

105

Navigation is difficult, the compass useless, the tides and currents uncharted, and the temperature only rises above freezing in July and August. Just six expeditions have completed the passage, and they have done so by taking an average of three years apiece to do it in. Charlie and I needed to get through the passage in under five weeks.

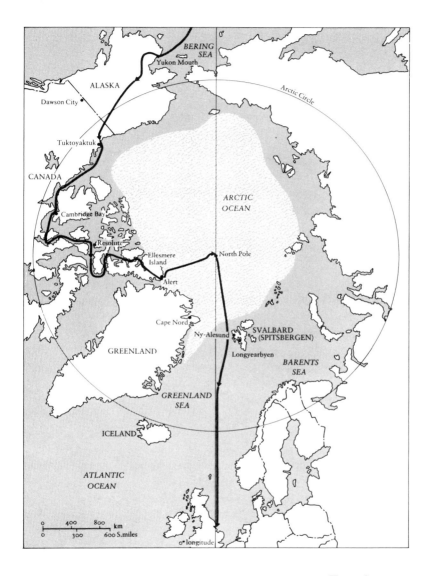

THE ARCTIC

107

7

Bothie in Love

GINNIE: There was no delaying at Tuktoyaktuk for Ran and Charlie. Even before I had set up my radio mast they were on their way, the whaler a diminishing shiny dot on the cold green Arctic Ocean. Simon, Bothie and I meanwhile were being given accommodation by the Polar Continental Shelf Project, first at their Tuktoyaktuk base and, when radio communication with the ice group dictated a move, we would shift to another of their bases at Resolute Bay. For the present our three strong team had a canvas hut beside the seashore. A bitter wind rattled by most days but Bothie found himself forced outside, despite his comfortable bed beside the radio nook. As soon as he was curled up there would be a low chuckling sound through the thin wall.

They were laughing at him again.

For a moment or two he would lie still, ears flicking and one eye opened with a look of longing that the mocking laughter would go away and leave him be. But his love of comfort, great though it was, was subjugated to that warrior spirit handed down through generations of Jack Russells. Such a challenge could not be ignored. And so, with a look of martyrdom, the noble hunter would shuffle off the delicious languor of his warm boudoir and yawn loudly. This meant "Open up!" and I would have to take off headphones, disentangle cables and try to hold the door ajar to let the dog out without the wind blowing paperwork all over the hut.

For a minute or so there would be ominous silence, then a brief chuckle followed by pandemonium, violent barking and a sound as of eight greyhounds leaving the starting gate. For an hour, sometimes more, battle would rage round and round the canvas hut. Brief lulls into silence would end with a new chuckle and more hoarse but hysterical barking. Eventually a scratching at the door, and a panting and bedraggled Bothie would droop into his bed. Within minutes, and as unremittingly as the next electricity bill, a new chuckle would sound ghost-like through the thin hut wall, this time tinged with gloating overtones.

On rare windless days and when radio watches allowed, I could sit on the doorstep and watch the fray. All about the hut were holes of the size found on golf courses, the numerous exits of the local gopher community. The gophers soon learnt that Bothie a) could not dig his way into their tunnel system, b) had fairly slow acceleration from the starting position due to wheel-spin on the dusty surface and, c) became increasingly unco-ordinated as his hysteria mounted. They themselves worked well together. I could never be sure how many there were in the colony but sometimes six adults would taunt Bothie from different holes at the same time and over the weeks that he lived in their midst they honed their tactics until the lone terrier must have reached the near edge of insanity. Their quaint squirrel faces, Disneyesque silhouettes, and endearing behaviour gave every appearance of their having truly lovable dispositions. But their latent evil was abundantly obvious to me after observing just one Bothie-taunting session.

At midday they liked to sleep, then at teatime to wake and converge on the canvas hut to draw out the terrier with a quick chuckle. Once their victim was outside, a predesignated gopher would nonchalantly leave his hole and amble into the open, seemingly unaware of the pop-eyed dog bunching its haunches to attack. Bothie was off, pounding towards the impudent gopher which, within inches of death, disappeared down a hole that just happened to open up right where needed. At some unseen signal two other gophers then began to stroll, chackering at each other, across the other end of the clearing. The terrier pounded again, with similar results, but no matter how often he drove the creatures below ground, an inexhaustible supply of new strolling, chuckling gophers paraded afresh just out of reach.

It was the stuff of Tantalus' nightmares and only got worse as the days went by and the tormentors, who seemed to love dicing with death, perfected their brinkgophership to the point where Bothie's gnashers clacked shut in mid-air within a whisker of the target gopher's backside. A strange thing happened that probably saved our hero from going round the twist. For the first time in his life he fell deeply in love.

At first the scavengers came purely out of hunger, having discovered the whereabouts of the camp kitchen door – not far from Bothie's hut. They were about a month old, black and covered with long fluffy hair. Their mother was an outsize Newfoundland, the father, it was locally thought, a pensioned-off husky-cum-Labrador. The liaison had been neither planned nor popular with the mother's owner, a local aircraft mechanic, and the puppies were to be shot if still unspoken for when weaned. Meanwhile they had to fend for themselves and twice daily returned to the kitchen door to share whatever they could find with the gophers.

Fed up to the back teeth with the damnable gophers,

Bothie went over to inspect the black puppies. They were sisters and very playful. Soon a happy friendship sprang up and the three dogs were to be seen all about the camp in single file or fighting playfully together. One day the prettier sister no longer came and I discovered the mechanic was soon to put down the remaining bitch which had a rather attractive squint like Rita Tushingham, but a squint nonetheless, which put off would-be foster parents.

By the time she was two months the remaining sister was nearly as large as Bothie. Simon's name for her was Toulouguk, which is Eskimo for 'black as a raven', and Bothie had become markedly possessive of her as soon as her sister disappeared. He began to invite her into the hut to share his bedspace.

"Out you get," shouted Simon. "Go on, git!"

"No," said I protectively, "let her stay. She's not doing any harm."

"She's hopping with fleas – which we'll catch."

"Where's a flea? Go on. Show me one!" I was indignant, although secretly suspecting Simon might be right.

When I later put it to him that I planned to adopt the black puppy, he had plenty to say, ending with a doleful prediction.

"You'll be far too busy to look after two dogs and I'll end up having to feed and clean up after the flea-ridden runt!"

"Rubbish," I said, knowing again that Simon was probably right, but by now committed to saving the bitch from an untimely end. In an unsuccessful attempt to placate Simon I took the black mangy creature to a tap on the wall and, with a bowl and my best shampoo, I gave her a thorough wash – noticing for the first time the size of her paws which were ginormous and webbed like a duck.

Early in August I began to have difficulty picking up

Ran's radio signals which were by then over a thousand kilometres away. They had been through many adventures including a near sinking by monster waves off cliffs which were permanently on fire from burning sulphur. On another occasion Ran had made an error with the polar bear gun and ended up with a hole in his chin and a fine set of stitches. On reaching the far flung settlement of Cambridge Bay the whaler ran into a wall of ice to the east, pack-ice which was liable to get worse not better, given the usual northerly winds. Cambridge Bay was also the refuelling stop for the PCSP Twin Otter taking Bothie and us from Tuktoyaktuk to Resolute Bay, our next base some 600 miles to its north.

Simon and I had stopped discussing the future of the black dog, and he finally became resigned when he read an airfreight list prepared for the PCSP Twin Otter. Listed casually under Bothie was the item: 1 x black dog . . . approx 15 lbs.

By the time the move was imminent Bothie was insepar-able from the now shiny but still scruffy puppy, to the extent that he would accompany her across his hut clearing and ignore even the most flagrant behaviour of the dis-gusted gopher clan.

RAN: When the aircraft touched down Ginnie came out with Bothie and, after greeting us, said quickly to me, "We have an extra dog. She's no problem and would have been shot if we had not brought her away from Tuktoyaktuk."

"Who's we?" I asked.

Simon was just behind Ginnie, but she could see there was going to be no support from that quarter. She switched quickly.

"I thought she would make a beautiful wedding present for Charlie."

"That's very thoughtful of you, Ginnie," said Charlie

Our camp at Tanquary.

Seeing off Ran and Charlie as they head north for the icefields of Ellesmere Island

firmly, "but Twink and I won't be needing any dogs for a long while yet."

"Well there's no problem. Resolute Bay is probably full of people who'll pay a mint to have a beautiful guard dog like this."

At that point a small all black Labrador puppy with a squint and outsize paws appeared in the Twin Otter doorway, its floppy tail wagging uncertainly. All those present were at that moment saying to themselves that, no matter how badly the citizens of Resolute might want the dog, there was no way Ginnie was likely to part with her and she was bound to end up with the black thing becoming a British citizen and a permanent fixture in the Fiennes household.

Ginnie quickly changed the subject, seeing the glum response the new item was receiving from everyone but Bothie, who was standing under the aircraft doorway, tail wagging furiously, and whining gently as he gazed lovingly up into the squinting brown eyes.

The Twin Otter's menagerie reboarded and left for Resolute. Charlie and I put canine superfluity aside and set out in a thick mist to attempt to travel 400 miles around the southern rim of the pack-ice.

GINNIE: At Resolute the hut which I was given to live in with the radios and the dogs was about six foot square. No room to swing a cat but extremely cosy and comfortable. Bothie was in seventh heaven for his new love shared his blanket and there were no gophers. Fearing I might become too attached to the black dog – for I had every intention of finding a home for her – I refused to call it Toulouguk or any other name. I referred to it merely as the 'black dog'.

In a short while Blackdog was the name she was answering to. But only I ever called it. Nobody in Resolute hankered after the squint-eyed puppy and indeed everyone tried to fill me with horrific visions of what she would grow up like. The more hostile people were, the more protective I became, but she *was* quite a handful and, quite apart from having a voracious appetite, was becoming what Simon liked to describe as ferocious with Bothie. She had grown very large all of a sudden and began to express her disapproval of his irritating twenty-four hour interest in her hind-quarters by snapping at him. He was naturally hurt by these rebuffs and had begun to sulk. So did the ionosphere.

Radio calls from the boat group sometimes failed to get through. Some days a weak message expressed optimism and hundreds of miles gained; at other times the position was hopeless with storms, fog and breakdowns threatening imminent failure. There were encounters with schools of beluga whales, with icebergs on dark nights, and foraging polar bears on lonely cliff-bound beaches. But good luck never seemed to abandon the little whaler and its crew who eventually made it to Resolute Bay.

The only channel from Resolute to the north was ice blocked which meant an additional 600-mile detour past the most exposed coastline in the Canadian Arctic. There was no choice so Ran and Charlie pushed, with little sleep, through seas of jostling icebergs and confusing fog until they passed by Hell Gate and came at last to the west side of Ellesmere Island. Their ultimate sea-borne goal was Tanquary Fjord in the north-west of the island and the PCSP Twin Otter was to take me there as soon as we heard they had reached Hell Gate.

Simon was to stay on at Resolute for a few days to wait for our own Twin Otter which Giles and Gerry were to fly across from England and then ferry supplies from Resolute to Alert, our home for the winter of 1981–2.

114

Simon actually *offered* to look after the black puppy until he came north. Suspicious of his motives though I was, I felt it would give Bothie time to recover his dignity after a particularly quarrelsome canine lovers' tiff, and so the two of us headed north.

Tanquary is my favourite place in the world. At the head of a long narrow fjord, it nestles serenely under the great mountains whose northern slopes reach down to the Arctic Ocean. Consisting of two canvas Parcol huts and a large aluminium warehouse, the settlement has been a centre for many scientific and adventurous groups seeking knowledge of the Ellesmere coastline. Within a few hours of arriving, the pilot who flew us up, an old-timer of the best possible sort, had lit the cooker in the kitchen and shown me where the soup and dried beef were to make some supper with. Bothie seemed to love this new environment where he could be left to roam freely and paddle in the little stream that provided fresh drinking water behind the hut.

"You had better keep an eye on the little fella," warned our friendly pilot as we walked with him to the plane. "There are wolves all around here and they'll be keen to know what the strange smell is."

Indignant I replied, "Bothie doesn't smell that bad!"

"No, but his pee does to the wolves. Just be careful, eh. And enjoy yourselves." With this warning he left, waggling the aircraft wings as he made a low swoop over our heads.

So I kept Bothie close to me as I worked around the camp in preparation for the arrival of Ran and Charlie. This was to be our secondary base for the aircraft during the next year's attempt at the North Pole and there was much to do.

After a supper of soup and reconstituted raspberries, I

left Bothie in the hut, apparently sleeping on a bed, whilst I went to light the stove in the other hut. They were awkward things when cold and it took longer than I thought. It was nearly 11.15 at night but still only dusk, when I heard Bothie barking excitedly. Frightened that the pilot's predictions had come true, I rushed out to see what was going on. To my relief he was down by the sea, leaping around on the thin layer of snow. I could see no wolves but the little devil would not respond when I called. He had obviously spotted something and was determined to tell me about it. I joined him on the shore and was dismayed to see that the water was greasy-looking. New frazil ice was forming on the surface.

Peering into the direction that Bothie seemed so interested in, I saw a tiny light. Slowly it came nearer and the shape of the whaler's hull was clear. They arrived, frozen stiff and dog tired, but in high spirits.

RAN: For the last 400 miles the boat broke through the new frazil ice which spread inexorably over the sea's surface. It was a fine race against time and we only won by a feather since, within forty-eight hours of the whaler reaching Tanquary Fjord, the inland channels to the south froze over and cut off any further movement by sea. Five great icecaps surround the head of Tanquary Fjord which is an idyllic spot and likely to remain that way so long as no precious minerals are found in the vicinity.

Two days later, Blackdog arrived to the delight of Bothie who, quick to forgive, took her around his new home in a proprietorial fashion. She was spreading out like Jack's beanstalk, especially her thick puppy legs which ended in the wide paws of a natural swimmer. Newfoundlands were originally bred to save drowning folk in the Newfoundland fishing communities.

At night wolves howled in the ravines which looked

116

down on the camp. It seemed, as time went by and the temperature dropped, that the howling increased and Ginnie began to notice wolves running around the edge of the camp even by day.

Although the howling wolves made Bothie uneasy, there were other new smells too tempting to ignore – musk-oxen, primordial buffalo with shaggy pile coats and aggressive horned heads that tapered to less impressive hind-quarters, travelled about the moss-covered bench-land above the camp in family bands from three to fifteen strong. White Arctic hares grazed in and about the camp and held boxing matches standing on their hind legs. They were pure white except for little black tips on their ears. They appeared to be larger than Bothie but most of their bulk was really just thick fur and both dogs chased them happily. Perhaps they reminded Bothie of Cat Franklin. Foxes, like lemmings and caribou, did not visit the camp, although they travelled within the fjord valley and left tracks on the sandbars.

GINNIE: Ran and Charlie trudged off to the north-east, stooped beneath heavy backpacks, and disappeared into a pass between two icecaps. After five days they had slowed down with raw blisters and Charlie had fallen and cut his head open on a rock. For a while they rested beside a lake then, using snowshoes, headed up into high snowfields which they must cross before a long descent to the edge of the Arctic Ocean, 150 miles away at Alert, our winter base.

There was less and less daylight at Tanquary and the wolves now seldom left the environs of the camp. They knew the two dogs were there and had seen them run loose, unaccompanied by humans. So they waited and grew bolder. I counted as many as seven wolves one night and was woken to find a large female staring through the

117

window of the hut. The dogs had sensed nothing and were sleeping quite unaware of the predatory visitor. White, very lean and Alsatian-sized, she quietly pulled their food bowl, a large old saucepan, away from the hut. I watched fascinated as this wonderful mother nervously pulled the pot to within forty yards of the hut where there were three young cubs waiting. She then sat by and kept watch as her half-starved young scraped and licked every morsel of food from the sides and bottom of the pot. The mother's own ribs showed clearly through her skin. With the cubs squabbling over the last lick of a pot, she looked around for further food. It was tempting to take some out but, knowing I would only be here for another few days, it seemed wrong to upset the delicate balance of nature. I will never know whether I was carrying the 'cruel to be kind' maxim too far, and am glad that on leaving the camp I did accidentally leave some meat and eggs and bread in a cooler box outside the kitchen.

On an unusually fine evening I left Blackdog in camp and went walking with Bothie to a nearby frozen stream bed. Hares stood up on their long hind-legs like frozen statues, bolting away as soon as Bothie gave token chase. On this occasion, for the hell of it, or perhaps aware that winter was just around the bend, Bothie scampered away towards the Redrock Glacier. He ignored my calls which grew shrill as I spotted two large wolves heading fast across a scree slope directly towards the terrier.

I scrabbled in my anorak pocket for the Smith and Wesson revolver, which I carried about the camp for just such emergencies as this, and fired off three shots in rapid succession. But this had no effect whatsoever on the wolves. God must have a special soft spot for Bothie, for the hare scent ended and the dog, losing interest, turned and scuttled back to me without ever noticing the wolves.

The following morning I was woken by Bothie, standing on my chest and the sound of baying right outside the door. On close inspection there was a very large male wolf, three other males, two females and four cubs. Looking through binoculars I could see others over towards the east. It was an eerie gathering of the pack. Bothie was uncertain what to do. He made funny nervous baying noises, quite unlike those he had learnt to do so well in Antarctica. Blackdog was scratching at the door. Because I had heard wolves were aggressive only to male dogs but unlikely to attack a human unless they were rabid or starving, I tied Bothie to the bed and left the hut cautiously with the bucket to collect stream water. The wolves stopped baying and slowly shuffled away, turning frequently to look at me, then continuing on their way.

For two days frequencies fluctuated wildly and I had great difficulty picking up Ran's evening signal. The Twin Otter arrived with Giles, Gerry and Simon and I prepared to move up to Alert. One evening Gerry and Simon took Blackdog for a walk along the beach where she found a dead fish two foot long. She picked up the stinking thing as Gerry bent to throw it back into the sea. A tug of war with much verbal abuse ensued, which left Gerry clutching a rotting tail and Blackdog gulping down the last morsel. Giles refused to allow the now evil smelling puppy into his plane for at least four days, so she was left to keep company with the by this time won over Gerry, as the Twin Otter first took Bothie and me to Alert, then continued with Simon to Resolute. He was to return to England for the winter.

Our final base that year, Alert, is the most northerly camp on earth. Ran and Charlie inched their way day by day over glaciers and along frozen riverbeds fully aware that they must reach Alert before the long darkness of the

Arctic winter closed in. The three huts into which Bothie and I moved were not only in need of a thorough clean, but were lined with hoar frost and the chimney pipes were choked with thick oily grime from the kerosene heaters. Within two days we were nearly as black as Blackdog.

On 26th September towards dusk Bothie pricked up his ears, sniffed the air and barked. Wearily I dropped my shovel and stared west, as I had done many times over the past week. This time I was rewarded by the sight of two dark and burdened figures descending the snowfield above the camp. The expedition had arrived at the edge of the Arctic Ocean in the nick of time. The long polar winter was about to begin.

Arctic hare, fun to chase; Arctic wolves, sensible to avoid.

Sunset for the Arctic winter over Alert.

Coffee break at Alert.

Looking north across the sea-ice toward the Pole.

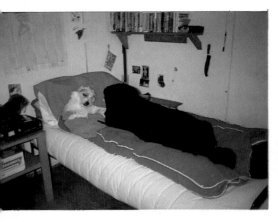 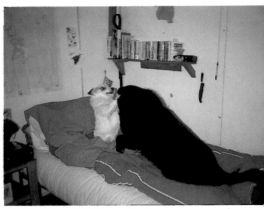

Contact sports on Ginnie's bed at Alert.

8

North Pole and Home

GINNIE: The Twin Otter made its last flight from Tanquary with equipment and Blackdog. Giles and Gerry returned to England, leaving us to sort out our polar equipment which had all arrived safely from Antarctica. The winter of 1981–2 passed by at Alert much as our southern Ryvingen months had but, without Ollie, life lost some of its zest. We could have done with his built-in buoyancy, for a sense of the enormity of what lay ahead affected us as soon as the sun disappeared.

RAN: Because our three wooden huts were within fifty yards of the coast and the mobile sea-ice, every new sound 'out there' took on a personal meaning for us. A sudden wind from the south would split the floes and through the darkness we would hear the unearthly roar of millions of tons of pack-ice on the move. It made us feel very small and glad that there were still four months in camp before we need set out over the hostile moving pack to our north.

In the camp I soon noticed that the black puppy Ginnie had briefly introduced back at Cambridge Bay was destined to be more than a handful. Already she was four times the size of Bothie and, far from following his lead, she now took him on tundra patrols round the edge of the camp. Her puppyhood depredations were worse than Bothie's had ever been, simply due to her size.

Snowdrifts enabled her to climb onto the hut roofs. She liked doing this and would pad about aimlessly above our heads which was maddening. I would hit the ceiling with a broomstick which got rid of her, but not for long. Ginnie's radio masts were situated in many parts of the camp but their coaxial cables all converged on our living hut-cum-radio shack. Ginnie had long ago learnt to keep cables at least three feet above snow level because Arctic foxes love to gnaw them – apparently to suck the salt and other minerals they find in them. But three feet was ideal for Blackdog since that was her mouth level. She soon discovered the delicious flavour and chewability of the cables, especially the highly expensive silicone-coated ones.

Many a time I heard Ginnie exclaiming furiously at some new communications failure caused by Blackdog and watched her hurl snowballs up onto the roof where the culprit lurked, grinning inanely and wagging her long tail about like the great oafish Newfie she was.

"Get rid of her now," I counselled Ginnie, as she bemoaned some new damage to her wiring circuit.

"I would if I could find a kind person to take her," she said, "but then again, she is so soft and adorable sometimes, and Bothie would be desolate without her."

"Try it and see. He'd probably be delighted. It was just youthful infatuation and now he's beginning to tire of her." Only the night before he had snarled at her as she got into his bed. All she did was ignore him, flop down on top of him and, when he struggled out from under her, she yawned, stretched her back legs and, in the process, kicked him onto the floor. "You know how proud he is. I tell you his dignity won't put up with her much longer. Nor will I if she destroys *one* more of my mukluks."

"Charlie and Simon love her," Ginnie said lamely.

"Rubbish!" I exploded. "You can say that safely about Simon now he's back in England, and won't be back for four months and you're quite wrong about Charlie. He won't even let her into his hut. Whereas Bothie's in there most days reading paperbacks on Charlie's bed and having his tummy scratched. Charlie's potty about him and can't stand that stupid squint eyed hulk."

At that moment the big Labrador puppy stood up in the dark outside and whined, pressing her soft face against the frosty window. Her squint had become far less pronounced and she did have a very sweet nature . . . but the sheer size of her was too much to contemplate. The thought of her monstrous black paws tearing up our square of lawn back in London made me shudder.

"Don't flap," said Ginnie reading my thoughts, "she's three months old now and probably fully grown."

A short while later, after the Arctic mongrel had performed an especially heinous act of destruction, Ginnie was forced to agree she must go and the sooner the better. I immediately contacted the major of the military camp, two miles to the south, and he promised to find a good foster parent for the dog from amongst his small garrison. Two days later he told us that a much respected flying sergeant was keen to take the dog home to his children as a Christmas present.

"That's it then, Ginnie," I said firmly. "I'll take her up to camp first thing tomorrow."

That night I caught Ginnie crying in bed and knew it was useless.

I phoned the sergeant up in the morning and apologised. "You know what women are like," I told him, "can't make up their minds . . . and she's besotted with the dog."

"Don't you worry, friend. Think nothing of it. Jes' you

give me a call if'n the missus changes her mind the other way agin in the next two days."

A kindly fellow I thought, *and* a lucky one.

That was the last time there was any mention of Blackdog leaving us. Bothie's chance pick-up was now part of the establishment.

GINNIE: I would like to mention one point in favour of the much maligned Blackdog. She once got shut in our tiny kitchen by mistake and, as we all know, puppy bladders are not strong. There was a flood to greet us and a very unhappy embarrassed Blackdog. She has *never* before or since had to be chastised for being incontinent (or just plain pig-headed like our wee Bothie). She was always a very clean, well behaved animal.

Christmas came and went with Bothie indulging himself more gluttonously than ever. A *huge* bone was sent him by our very amiable neighbours, the Canadians, with a big red bow tied to it. Blackdog had a large bag of T-bone steak bones. T-bones all devoured, she sat drooling at her admirer as he gnawed on his bone. After many hours he rested, at first guarding his treasure by snarling if she dared move a muscle, but finally he moved away and thereby notifying his canine friend that she could have a go. She made short work of one knuckle before Charlie removed the bone and put it out of reach until Bothie might want it again.

Blackdog took no offence and asked, with a gentle stroke of her massive furry paw, to be allowed out. She returned within twenty minutes, with a black 'thing' in her mouth. It looked odd and smelt revolting. But she was obviously proud of it as she held her head high, her tail wagging in wild circles before placing it between Bothie's front paws. A Christmas present perhaps for a true friend. Bothie appeared touched by the gesture, but was still exhausted from his strenuous efforts with the bone, so the two dogs breathed deep sighs and curled up together under the table.

RAN: Ginnie heard that there were to be five other expeditions during the coming spring, all intending to reach the North Pole and some, like us, to go on and cross the Arctic Ocean. As it turned out they all failed except the Norwegians who did reach the Pole. But awareness of this competition strengthened our determination to set out as early as possible. No previous expedition had ever crossed the Arctic Ocean in a single season. Our logistics made it imperative that we do so, or accept failure after many years of work.

No man, not even Admiral Peary and his Eskimos, had ever set out towards the Pole before the end of February at the very earliest. Anything earlier is considered suicidal, since to move in darkness and extreme cold on the Arctic Ocean is asking for trouble. It is treacherous terrain, so totally unlike Antarctica, an unpredictable, ever-fracturing ice skin that moves ceaselessly over the surface of the fifth largest ocean on earth. Since the North Pole was less than half-way across the total distance involved and since, even with the beefy presence of Ollie, we had failed to reach it on our earlier training bid, our chances now did not look good.

However, since failure to complete the crossing seemed more likely should we wait for sun-up in early March, we decided to take the risk and leave Alert in early February.

GINNIE: There was much to be done in the six weeks before their departure. Throughout the winter we had anxiously kept a check on the temperature and on the ice depths in the bay. Theoretically from early November the ice should have started to become thicker as the cold temperatures, normal for the winter months, froze the sea water deeper and deeper. This is what we needed to make for a safer surface on which to travel. But it didn't happen in the winter of 1981–2. All November was very mild, sometimes reaching −15°C or −18°C. Before Christmas we were experiencing ridiculously warm temperatures between −9°C and −11°C, whereas our families and friends at home in England were having a terrible winter with temperatures ranging to −25°C in some parts. The meteorologists at the military camp explained that there was a 'reversal in the jet streams' somewhere over the Greenland icecap causing this phenomenon.

The sea-ice did not really begin to freeze that winter until mid-March when the temperatures dropped dramatically. But this was too late to start building the good firm thickness there would have been if it had started freezing during the winter darkness. (In early March an aircraft from Resolute reported more open water north of our camp and across the north coast of Greenland than they had ever seen.)

The three of us knew the Arctic to be a more unforgiving and harsh environment than Antarctica or the North-West Passage and, had it not been for the distractions of work to be done and the dogs, I would have become hopelessly nervous of saying goodbye to Ran and Charlie.

While we were busy Bothie and Blackdog were largely left to amuse themselves, which they seemed happiest doing. They found endless delight in seeking out the white hares that delved beneath the snow to scrape lichen from the frozen ground, or the small white half-crazed Arctic foxes that had dug homes under our huts. At times Bothie could be seen staring in amazement as Blackdog chased fantasies in the deep powder snow, pouncing from one place to another like a comical panther, digging huge pits in the snow like something possessed, or sniffing loudly along the shoreline at the tide cracks in the sea-ice. When her antics became too fanciful for Bothie to stomach he would come to find one of his human friends and throw a ball at them to initiate a more civilised game. He had become very demonstrative in his old age and if he got no immediate attention he would half whine-half growl, and stamp his front paws impatiently on the ground, first left then right, until he got satisfaction.

RAN: Blackdog discovered nine lonely gravestones, the site of an air crash, a mile above our camp. From there she roamed, taking Bothie with her, to the Canadian airstrip and managed to embarrass Ginnie by greeting the arrival of the weekly mail/groceries Hercules in the midday darkness. The airstrip was out-of-bounds to anyone or anything that might endanger the dicey winter landings and take-offs. Ginnie had to give the station commander a solemn promise it would not happen again.

GINNIE: Confined to barracks, they developed games in the huts. Bothie's old Antarctic ball-in-a-sock and tug-the-bone games were rekindled. These soon developed into tug-the-sock between the two dogs, Bothie doing all the tugging, and Blackdog holding her end so effortlessly that she sometimes got bored with the game and let go, catapulting the unsuspecting Bothie across the hut. At other times the game grew wild. Boxes stacked high with equipment went flying, or the sock would get wrapped round a table leg before trundling across the hut, with papers, equipment, mugs of coffee, spilling all over the floor.

We discovered we all had one thing in common with Blackdog at least. She, too, found Bothie's habit of dropping his ball – *boing, boing, boing, boing* – across the bare boards to attract attention particularly irritating when she was trying to sleep. When she could bear it no longer she would drag herself from her bed, pick up the ball, drop it in the middle of the bed, then lie on top of it. Bothie would sit distraught two foot from the massive black bulk. Having learnt it was useless to try and push her off or dig underneath her, he would use all his psychic powers to try to levitate her off his best ball.

RAN: The black mutt unearthed a long-forgotten incineration pit below our camp. She seemed to be able to dig down through permafrost with her dozer-like paws and dredged up a trove of half-burnt tins of Canadian Army corned beef. This must have been condemned many years back and was now greenish-black. She would bring a tin quietly into Ginnie's bed and, clasping it between her forepaws, somehow would puncture it without hurting her soft jowls, then remove the contents piece by stinking piece by delicately inserting a long tongue. In the warmth of the hut, the aged meat soon gave out a repulsive smell as from a flyblown corpse and Ginnie, leaping from her radio work, would chase the horrible dog, tin in mouth, into the outer darkness.

Somehow such filthy habits did not dim the love that Bothie still bore Blackdog, a love that was kindled afresh when she came on heat for the first time. Bothie had not the first idea what to do about it, but followed her everywhere, his nose just four inches from her tail, day after day out across the frozen bay and who knows where. He was in a total trance, returning zombie-like when she did, bumping into her when she stopped suddenly. He refused to eat, drink or sleep but sat all night howling gently, between bouts of shivering, outside the straw-strewn kennel where Ginnie locked Blackdog by night. Soon he was so tired he'd nod off on his feet, and so emaciated that we grew concerned about him. We couldn't *make* him eat, but we tried to make him sleep by forcing half an aspirin down his throat and shutting him in our

Ran could just imagine her digging up the lawn back home.

Tug-the-sock was an uneven contest.

Blackdog trying to look at home inside Bothie's bed-box.

bedroom. It worked for three hours, until he staggered over to the door and sat whimpering for the rest of the night asking to go and join her.

Departing from Alert proved to be the most difficult of our farewells. There was no ceremony. At noon on Friday 13th February, with the skidoos we had used in the south and heavy laden sledges, Charlie and I left the camp. Ginnie wore a brown wolfskin parka, tears froze on her cheek. Blackdog stood broad, black and gormless. Bothie, almost too small and too white to see, keened softly to himself as they stood silently in a pool of lamplight, their breath forming frost-laden wraiths.

GINNIE: Ran said goodbye to me and fondly patted both dogs. Charlie, with no human loved one to witness his going, had lingered with Bothie, his good friend and confidant throughout that anxious winter.

When the sound of the engines was quite gone into the night, Blackdog sniffed Bothie's nose, then jumped up, nearly flattening me as she put her massive paws on my shoulders and looked questioningly into my eyes. Bothie knew what it was all about – he had been through it before, but Blackdog was confused. For four days we kept radio watch, refuelled generators, and tidied up the camp in readiness for the Twin Otter crew and Simon who would arrive any time now. It was ghostly quiet and lonely but for the foxes who scrabbled under the hut at night and my two companions, although even they were somewhat subdued. Blackdog had the decency not to eat any critical part of the communications network and Bothie would come over and nudge my elbow, asking to be picked up. After a wet kiss on ear or chin he would curl up in my lap and be comforted by a tummy scratch.

The Twin Otter was delayed in England by engine troubles which Gerry could not locate. Then he developed stomach troubles himself and went into hospital. Our pilot for the north was Karl Z'Berg, a Swiss Canadian with unrivalled experience of flying over the Arctic Ocean. We had first met him and grown to trust him implicitly during our training in 1977 and were overjoyed when he agreed to join the team for this period. Karl knew we were anxious to have the aircraft at Alert as soon as possible and, as he had been an aircraft engineer before a pilot, he volunteered to take care of this side of things too until Gerry was fit to join us.

Bothie perked up his ears and rushed out of the radio hut when he recognised the drone of the Twin Otter coming in to land. We went up to the airstrip to greet them – Bothie sitting on my knee with his forepaws resting on the handlebar of the skidoo and, her husky instincts no doubt coming to the fore, Blackdog running, as she always liked to, just two inches in front of the vehicle ski.

Karl made the first flight to the ice group, leaving Alert to arrive with them as the sun was giving maximum light on the thin fragile ice. The landing was unpleasant and dangerous, but he gave Ran and Charlie the light pulk sledges they needed to continue. They had had to abandon their skidoos and were now manhauling basic supplies north at a rate of two to three miles per sixteen-hour day. The vehicles had been unable to cope with the chaos of ice rubble, including thirty-five-foot high walls of ice blocks pushed up by the pressure of wind and current.

Back in the camp Bothie and Blackdog made friends with Karl and took every opportunity to sneak after him up the hill to the airstrip. This was annoying for Karl as, after trudging through the snow for fifteen minutes, he would discover the two hounds at his heels, and have to turn round and march them back to camp. One morning he didn't notice them and, on reaching the airstrip, they decided to see what lay further up the hill. Following the road, they marched in single file into the Canadian military camp, past the officers' mess, the sergeants' and other ranks', past the gym and, inevitably, to the back door of the canteen – 'THE MOST NORTHERLY CANTEEN IN THE WORLD', 'IN THE LAND OF THE NOONDAY MOON' the placard read, or in summer, 'THE LAND OF THE MIDNIGHT SUN'. The menu board outside offered moose and caribou steaks and 'Lemming Meringue Pie'. Here the dogs sat and waited. Instead of the door opening and a moose steak being thrown to them, the door opened and a burly Canadian fell over them. It didn't take long to work out where the two mongrels had come from and they were duly returned under military escort. Fortunately the Canadian station commander had a sense of humour and gave the dogs full marks for initiative, but it meant another enforced period confined to barracks.

Karl spent many miserable cold hours cramped in the aircraft's tail section, sifting carefully through the complicated electronics and wiring, trying to solve the great engine failure mystery. After nearly two solid days and nights he arrived in the radio hut, his face drawn and grey but he allowed himself a little chuckle of well earned satisfaction as he described the fault he'd found and corrected. This good news cheered us all and, with the sun slowly creeping a bit further over the horizon each day, life seemed to be improving.

A message came through in early March that the rubble was getting less and the ice group now wished to try using two small skidoos. Simon worked late into the night to prepare the vehicles and left them in the garage to prevent their freezing up. At 0310 hours, after twenty-one hours of anxious radio watches, I closed down after the hourly standby call to the ice group, and went to bed. This was

quite a struggle since, following Ran's departure, both
Bothie and Blackdog had taken to sleeping on my bed,
leaving very little room. However, dog tired and begirt by
dogs, I went out like a light. At breakfast time we were to
have another weather check to Ran and, all being well,
Karl would fly the skidoos out to them.

Inside the garage was *everything* the expedition might
require to keep Ran and Charlie going. Tools, rations,
special light bridging gear, fur parkas, rubber boats, spare
parts for skidoos, navigation and scientific equipment and
apart from hundreds of other smaller items, the two
skidoos and loaded sledges needed that morning out on
the ice. Also inside the hut were boxes of phosphorous
flares, 7.62 rifle ammunition, acid batteries, aerosols and
other explosive materials, whilst just outside the up-wind
wall, were twelve forty-five gallon drums of petrol, left there
many years before, and now frozen deep into the ground.

Soon after 0325 hours my brain, totally befuddled by
sleep, responded to an alarm bell fixed up not long before
by the thoughtful Canadians. Their night watch had seen
a red glow. Was everything OK with us? Trying to focus
sleep-hooded eyes, I soon wished I hadn't. There *was* a
red glow and it was clearly visible through the garage
window. Also, I realised suddenly, the radios and lights
that were left on at all times were not on.

Forgetting the man on the end of the line, forgetting I
only had bedclothes on, I grabbed a fire extinguisher,
rushed into the cold night air and fell headlong into the
snowbank outside the door. Screaming "Fire!" I slithered
up the icy slope to the garage and flung open its main
sliding door, my only thought to pull out the skidoos and
sledges which were going to Ran and Charlie in a few
hours. It was hopeless. I was confronted by a curtain of
flame. The extinguisher was about as useful as a gnat

piddling in a bonfire. I threw it away. Night blinded by the glare of the flames and still screaming "Fire!" I tried to reach another entrance as the whole side wall frizzled up and caved in.

Simon and Karl were both still sound asleep as I burst desperately into their hut. Never before and (I hope for his sake, never again) has Simon left his bed so quickly. He was out shovelling snow in an instant. Karl, with unpleasant experiences of several fires in Arctic camps, was more practical than us and hastily removed an armful of vital things from his hut before joining the snow shovelling effort. Too many times he had been caught out, losing everything he possessed and nearly losing companions in a camp that had not woken in time as a fire took its greedy hold. The extraordinarily dry atmosphere in the polar regions makes everything like tinder and once a fire starts there is little hope of containing it.

"Where are the dogs?" Karl asked.

Of the Arctic bitch, she of brave husky strain, there was not a sign nor a whimper. In fact she managed to disappear for two whole days and nights before being discovered cowering under Charlie's old hut, the building furthest away from the conflagration. Bothie on the other hand realised the fire was an enemy. Not being a dab hand with extinguisher or shovel he did the best he could. He faced the ever-spreading inferno and cantered round and round it so close that he singed his fur, yapping with all the ferocity he could muster. By dawn he had lost his voice, but still kept going.

Simon, Karl and I rescued what we could of the boxes stacked against the burning hut, but every item inside was totally destroyed. The ammunition exploded. So too did the fuel drums which spewed flaming petrol and black clouds high into the air. As each drum exploded with a deep boom Bothie leapt into the air too, retaliating with an extra fierce, but now voiceless, bark.

The ice group continued to manhaul. The aircraft was safe from damage by the fire. I borrowed two large batteries from the Canadians to run the radios to keep up the radio contacts. After two or three days and a fall of snow the debris was cool enough to walk amongst to list what we could recognise for insurance purposes. We never did discover the cause of the fire. Simon reckoned it must have been a fault in the wiring.

Blackdog reappeared some days later and risked sniffing around the edge of the black mess, finding to her delight that there were tins which, if punctured, contained the most delicious cooked biscuits, spam, cheese and meat. She was then content to spend day after day rifling through the charred remains scavenging what she could. She found a whole pile of tins which had once been Pedigree Chum. These were particularly appetising and she hid many of them under the hut for later consumption.

We managed to replace enough equipment from our Tanquary base for the ice group to continue but they were soon slowed to a mere northerly teeter and Ran, blinded by blowing snow, drove his skidoo into a canal of icy sludge, whilst trying to avoid another one. He was flung clear but skidoo, sledge and vital equipment sank quickly to the ocean floor. For forty-eight hours they suffered unbearable conditions with one sleeping bag, no tent and only emergency food. Comatose with cold, they sang to keep from falling asleep. Karl managed to get to them with minimal gear and they limped on. Time was now against them for the sun was high and the pack-ice had begun its relentless summer melt.

Gerry arrived, still suffering from a hiatus hernia, and we were also joined by 'Flo' (Laurence Howell) who I had come to know well over the radio in Antarctica where he was a radio operator at one of the British bases. He was to man the base at Tanquary Fjord.

A week later a series of snowstorms raged through the camp at Alert and a violent squall snapped the ropes that tethered the Twin Otter, tipping it over to smash one wing tip. The media around the world sensed imminent failure and made hay with such headlines as 'Polar expedition in flames', followed by 'Expedition leader sinks', and now 'Team cut off in race to Pole'. Whilst I desperately needed to use every minute on the radio to get resupplies of equipment and make other urgent calls to our London office, the press wanted interviews. "When will they be brought back?" "How will they be brought back?" "Is there any search and rescue facility to collect them?"

It was difficult to get them to understand that they were *not* coming back – they were going to go on. One evening I was so tired and so helpless with frustration with one journalist that I grabbed Bothie and held a ball high in the air, guaranteed to make him bark. Then I pressed the microphone. A mystified journalist decided he had a crossed line and gave up.

Karl and Gerry somehow managed to fix up the Twin Otter wing and completed a resupply drop which kept the ice group slowly axing their way through March and April until, early on Easter Sunday, Ran's voice, clear but tired announced, "We've gone 7.2 miles and have reached 90° north. We're here. There's no-one to meet us but we're here."

Bothie had been sleeping on my lap. He gargled a snarl as he was hurled into the air and caught. Indignantly he shook himself, then realised something *really* needed urgent celebration. They were the first men ever to reach both Poles over the surface of the earth. With Bothie yakkering, I rushed out into the snow and leaping up and down, yelled for all to hear – "They've arrived!"

The kitchen door burst open. The others appeared and a cheer went up. Blackdog stood there, mouth agape in disbelief at the scene. Her whole world, including Bothie, had gone quite mad. Back in the radio hut I could hear animated chatter, singing and other not normally accepted radio procedure as our faraway ship's crew rejoiced with Ran and Charlie.

RAN: The camp celebrations that day temporarily camouflaged concern about the immediate future. We had arrived at the top of the world a lot later than planned, and we were not yet half-way across an ocean whose rapidly fracturing ice skin would soon stop us moving other than by camping on a solid-looking floe and hoping it would drift in the general direction of England rather than Siberia. Our ship was still a thousand miles away and halted by a barrier of ice.

Such worries about our future did not deter the *Daily Mirror* from chartering a Twin Otter at great expense and flying all the way to the North Pole. Their ski-plane touched down on the only flat strip near the Pole which was along a corridor of suspiciously thin new ice. Karl landed within twenty minutes in our own Otter on the same strip bringing in a film crew, David Mason, Simon and Bothie. Bothie, determined to be on film as the only dog to have stood at both Poles, left his mark, not once but several times, at the base of our Union Jack – which we were not entirely happy about. Since there were no other vertical objects in the vicinity he was forgiven.

The pilots were keen to be away as soon as possible and both 'planes disappeared behind the horizon of jumbled ridges, not a moment too soon, as the crackle of new fracturing sounded from the area of the airstrip.

A Christmas musk ox bone from the Canadians.

Blackdog liked to explore the tide crack along the shoreline.

Blackdog resists chewing the delectable silicone-coated radio cables.

Simon, Karl and Gerry unloading the Twin Otter at Alert.

Our hut is destroyed.

Is it all going to end in disaster?

Easter 1982 at the North Pole, with David Mason, Charlie, Ran, Karl and Simon.

A dog for all seasons.

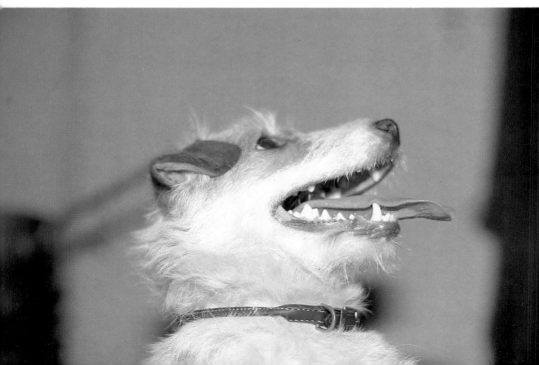

Charlie and I headed south, aiming for Soviet Franz Josef Land, but in the hope the Transpolar Drift current would help sweep us down between Greenland and Spitsbergen into Fram Strait where the *Benjamin Bowring* would spend the summer waiting. The longer the summer break-up held off, the greater our chance of getting within range of the ship in time.

GINNIE: Back at Alert hot soup and 'Gerry-special' stew awaited the returning passengers and crews. During the feast, made so by a bottle of champagne from our London office, Simon joked with the *Mirror* men.

"You know Bothie doesn't like journalists. He'll soon turn nasty if you don't give him some titbit. It's only the general excitement that has made him forget your existence here."

David Mason nudged the hound under the table as the *Mirror* man said, "Nonsense, we're great friends, aren't we, Bothie?"

As he leant forward to pat the terrier, David surreptitiously pointed his long finger in silence, and Bothie, catching sight of that never to be forgotten finger out of the corner of his eye let out an uncharacteristically vicious snarl that had a terrified *Mirror* man hurtling backwards, quite deflated and most upset. Often thereafter Karl was to be found, creased up with laughter, as he experimented with the finger-technique which turned the otherwise bubbling terrier into a snarling, never-to-be-taken-for-granted beast.

May is a period of frequent sea mists over the Arctic Ocean and Alert being especially prone to fog, we needed the Tanquary airstrip manned. David Mason and our Antarctic radio operator, Flo, were dropped off there and soon attracted a goodly company of Bothie's old friends, the wolves. When David had to return to England, Flo stayed on alone. One day he forgot to take his pistol when visiting the isolated lavatory shack and was marooned for over an hour by a posse of adult wolves before he dared a dash to the safety of the main hut.

Flo and I were now permanently on watch from Alert and Tanquary. The distance to the ice group was only 500 miles but radio conditions at that time were dismal and we were forever changing antennae and frequencies in our attempt to keep contact. For Karl too the long lonely flights over the frozen sea-ice were made more unpleasant and risky by the fluctuating radio conditions. The knowledge that the annual ice break-up was imminent did not help our peace of mind. Bothie seemed to sense the anxiety and stayed beside me, despite the temptations of fox-hunting with his black lover. Ten weeks after their departure from Alert Ran and Charlie came to a halt some 200 miles on the far side of the Pole.

RAN: I decided to search for an ice floe thick enough to weather the break up and float hundreds of miles to the south amidst the enormous lateral pressure of the moving pack. When we found one we set up our two-tent camp in the centre of this natural raft and prepared to take our chances. For if prevailing winds did not blow strongly to the south for the next three months the two of us would still be miles from the reach of the ship by the time the pack-ice solidified again at summer's end.

In mid-May the ship, with her original crew, battled her way to the Spitsbergen fjord of Adventsdalen but could go no further north. In June she battered a route another hundred miles into the ragged edges of the pack but retired with cracked welding in her bows. It seemed as though the expedition must fail at the last fence. In London it was suggested that Karl should evacuate us from our rapidly disintegrating floe. We were reluctant to do this and, anyway, within days the floe was a cullender of drain holes and melt pools where no 'plane could possibly land. We were now totally dependent on the whim of wind, current and fate.

GINNIE: Bothie detected tenseness between us all in the base. He might have expected the sun's return to make people happy, as it had in Antarctica, but, no, everybody was on tenterhooks. Even Gerry was not his normal cheerful self. At coffee time one morning he was totally disgusted as he saw Bothie climb onto the dining table and steal a half pound pat of butter in front of his very eyes. He decided the shameless dog needed a refresher course in flying lessons and, opening the door, pro- pelled the terrier, butter and all, off his boot into the snow.

Quite unrepentant, Bothie picked himself up, shook the snow from his coat and was about to take himself off with his butter to some more peaceful place when he spotted two huskies, both adolescent females, coming down the hill. Now even Blackdog lost her cool as she saw these two wayward wenches approach *her* dog. They were both on heat and caused a great furore during the following two days, as Bothie suddenly turned from a well behaved, respectful and perhaps naive one-bitch dog into a randy, oversexed philanderer. The episode was too horrific to print but did result in the two huskies being removed forcibly from our camp and Blackdog never again, deep down, quite trusting in Bothie's faithfulness.

One foggy morning I called the two dogs into the radio room and kneeling on the floor with them tried to explain that Simon, Karl, Gerry and I must go away from Alert and this time they could not come too, but must go back with Flo to England and spend six months in quarantine kennels. I made all sorts of promises about visiting them just as soon as the expedition was over. I hugged the dogs, my head buried between them, the black silk of Blackdog and the white fluff of Bothie – a real friend with whom I'd been through so much and whom I would miss terribly. It seemed such a rotten thing to send them off, but I had no choice. Sobbing, I made them a special meal of the last of the steaks and some doggy sedative and gave them over to the care of Flo.

On arrival at Heathrow Airport the dogs found themselves celebrities. There was Flo and David Mason and a great many strange people who flashed cameras at them. Bothie knew all about cameras and made off to the back of the cage. A curt order from David soon had him back, sitting to attention beside Blackdog who had flopped down mesmerised by the popping lights, her puppy squint temporarily reactivated by the flashes, and in the evening newspapers she looked decidedly Japanese. A locked van approved by the Ministry of Agriculture and Fisheries drove the celebrities to the Ruislip quarantine kennels where the proprietors, Joe and Liz Cartledge, showed them to their quarters and a slap-up dinner.

The weeks and months that followed were not, it is true, as exciting as expedition life. For Blackdog, who had never smelled such strange things as grass and tarmac before, there were initial surprises but these soon wore off. The Cartledges were kind and on one occasion even invited both dogs up to the house to watch television. Poor Bothie couldn't work out the cause of all the excitement when people pointed at the screen and told him, "Look, they've made it to the ship. That's your master in the red jacket. Don't you recognise them?" But when the set was turned off cold sausages were circulated, so from Bothie and Blackdog's point of view the visit was not a complete waste of time after all.

On the 29th August, Bothie's favourite kennel maid brought him a newspaper.

"Look, Bothie," she said, squatting beside him and pointing at a large picture of the expedition ship in the middle of the River Thames. "They're back in England. Now they'll come and see you. Won't that be lovely."

There came the furious snarling of a dog fight nearby. The kennel maid rushed out of Bothie's cage, leaving behind the paper which Bothie used in the manner we had long and ardently encouraged.

A week later Ran and I appeared at the cage and there was much cuddling of an at first curiously docile Bothie.

"Do you think he still knows who we are?" I asked Ran anxiously, scratching the brown patch by Bothie's ear.

"Maybe," said Ran. "Difficult to tell."

Ran picked up the six-inch soft ball we had brought to see if he remembered any of his tricks. He threw it at Bothie saying, "Catch!" Far from bouncing it back off his nose with that familiar clashing of teeth, Bothie stopped as if he'd seen a ghost; then with tail wagging so hard his backside shook, he leapt up at Ran, then at me, and smothered us both with big wet kisses.

"I think he does recognise us after all," we laughed.

So for three more months Bothie the delinquent, the Wooza, the Wooz Pog – the super dog; and Blackdog the goofy Newfie girlfriend, stayed in their cages and were visited by us and other old friends. Then on a lovely October day a mass of press people descended on the kennels and again the dogs sat, begged and grinned for the cameras. Bothie performed his repertoire of ball games for BBC News, for 'Blue Peter' and for 'This is Your Life', then the cages were unlocked. The dogs were free and, with their licences, collars and name-tags, they were taxpaying British citizens and free to go.

Within a few days Blackdog had settled down in suburban London, where she learnt the intense pleasure to be had from digging great holes in the lawn at night, and aiding and abetting our hero in chasing Cat Franklin by day. If ever she yearned for the snows of Tuktoyaktuk she has never shown it.

We held a welcome home party for Bothie and Blackdog with a barbecue in the garden. The lawn already resembled the Somme in 1918, but one could skirt the craters. Many of Bothie's friends were away but Ollie arrived with a raw mutton bone as large as his arm and the steward of the *Benjamin Bowring* with a supply of rubber chews. Anton was there and the bosun, too. We all drank a toast to Bothie and the long line of venturesome Jack Russells we hoped he would one day sire (preferably not by Blackdog). Bothie snarled impressively over his giant mutton bone as Ollie, unperturbed by the big bluff, knelt beside him, knowing full well that Bothie was all mouth and no trousers, and scratched that favourite patch on his back.

After that Bothie developed quite a flair for public relations. There were tours around London with magazine photographers – Bothie beside Nelson's Column (upper lip curling at the nearby pigeons), Bothie on the quay beside Scott's *Discovery* (looking unimpressed), Bothie at the Tower of London, Madame Tussauds and so on. Posters were printed from colour slides of the terrier in his red jacket looking nobly into the distance at Ryvingen. Fluffy life-size Bothies were sold at Harrods and Hamley's. He opened village fêtes and county dog shows, appeared on 'Blue Peter' and with Russell Harty whom he growled at and tried to nip on the thigh.

Pedigree Petfoods, whose provender had sustained him for three years around the world, gave him a final consignment but Blackdog, now fully grown, ate three-quarters of it.

Bothie was voted Pet of the Year 1982, visited Pringle, the Emperor penguin at Chessington Zoo, won the Heineken Christmas Award and broke *all* precedents when the Chairman of the Kennel Club invited him to 'do a circuit' and present a prize at the 1983 Crufts Dog Show.

RAN: Ginnie accompanied the terrier, all too aware that only pedigree dogs, creatures of nobility, beauty and impeccable lineage, *ever* trotted their dainty way about that hallowed ring. She swore at Bothie under her breath as he tugged sideways towards the leg of a ring-side St Bernard and when he tried to stop beside a flagpole. Somehow they made it out of the ring without disgracing the good name of Jack Russell. A mongrel he undoubtedly was and a stubborn-minded, non-housetrained, contrary-souled, yappy-voiced one at that. But he was also Bothie who had made us laugh, given us something to love and talk to during those long difficult months.

Sometimes when the winter wind rattles the windows, Ginnie shoves a log on the fire and Blackdog, covering the entire surface of the sofa, rolls over, sighs deeply and revives her dreams, tail and toes twitching. Bothie will look up at us, his brown eyes soft but questioning. Perhaps he is trying to say, "When are we off again to the great white places beyond the seas, to high adventures fit for a polar dog?"